# ARISE
## A 40-Day Journey for Women

Melodi Hawley

D1367962

CITY ON A HILL

PRESS

# Arise
## A 40-Day Journey for Women
Melodi Hawley

Copyright @ 2017 City on a Hill Press
Print ISBN: 978-0-9993412-0-9
e-Book ISBN: 978-0-9993412-1-6

*To my beautiful daughters, Eden, Zia, and Chanyn
and the women of I Heart Church*

*May God use a bunch of girls to change the world!*

# ARISE

Is it possible to really rise
From this place of depravity?
Is it possible to really rise
From this place of obscurity?

Is it possible?

Is it possible to really rise
When I've been down in this pit so long?
Is it possible to really rise
When I've been wounded? When I've been wronged?

Is it possible?

But from the distance, I can hear
Oh, from the eastern sky,
From the distance, I can hear
Echoes of heaven's reply!

He says, "ARISE!"
He says, "ARISE!"
Oh, girl, God says to you, "ARISE!"

It's cold down here, down in this pit
But Jesus said that this ain't it!
I know it's cold down here, down in this pit
But Jesus said that this ain't it!

He says, "ARISE!"
He says, "ARISE!"
Oh, girl, God says to you, "ARISE!"

# CONTENTS

FOREWORD .................................................................I

AWAKE, ARISE, & SHINE ...............................................1

VISION DAY.................................................................5

    DAY 1. CLUMSY LIKE ME .......................................5

THE AWAKEN PHASE...................................................11

    DAY 2. SPILLED MILK, BROKEN LIVES....................13
    DAY 3. JUNKYARD VALLEY ...................................17
    DAY 4. THE VACANT ROOM DOWN THE HALL ..........21
    DAY 5. BABY FINGERS.........................................27
    DAY 6. THIS OLD HOUSE .....................................31
    DAY 7. I WANT AN ORANGE NOSE ........................35
    DAY 8. THROWING ANTS AT BOYS.........................39
    DAY 9. CAN I TELL YOU A SECRET? .......................43
    DAY 10. DON'T FUSS BETWEEN BITES ....................49
    DAY 11. EYE EXAM .............................................53
    DAY 12. STICKY TRAP ..........................................57
    DAY 13. PLAYING CHURCH ...................................63
    DAY 14. GRAB THE CORD!.....................................69

THE ARISE PHASE.......................................................73

    DAY 15. THE SOUND AN APPLE TREE MAKES .........75
    DAY 16. WHAT'S YOUR KRYPTONITE?.....................79
    DAY 17. MONKEY-SEE, MONKEY-DO .....................83
    DAY 18. CAN YOU HEAR ME NOW? .......................87
    DAY 19. SHOO FLY!.............................................91
    DAY 20. SHOO FLY!.............................................97
    DAY 21. BENJAMIN BUTTON CHRISTIANITY .........103
    DAY 22. THE BEST BLANKIE EVER .......................109
    DAY 23. BUT FIRST, LET ME TAKE A #SELFIE .........113
    DAY 24. COOKING UP A PLAN TO SIN ...................119
    DAY 25. MY KNEES ARE HURTING! ......................123
    DAY 26. MY QUITE UN-FABULOUS TODAY ............127
    DAY 27. THE FIVE-MINUTE WARNING....................133

THE SHINE PHASE.....................................................137

    DAY 28. HOLY BLING...........................................139
    DAY 29. SWITCHING TREADMILLS.........................143
    DAY 30. WASHERS, DRYERS, & THE CHRISTMAS SPIRIT .....147
    DAY 31. WHEN IS "ENOUGH" ENOUGH? ................151

DAY 32. No One Likes a Brat ..................................................... 155
DAY 33. God's Secret Weapon................................................ 159
DAY 34. A Different Way to Shine ........................................... 163
DAY 35. Shining in Suffering.................................................. 169
DAY 36. Hey There, Darlin'..................................................... 173
DAY 37. This Little Light of Mine ........................................... 177
DAY 38. Breaking the Fourth Wall ....................................... 181
DAY 39. A New Journey Begins ............................................. 185
DAY 40. Broadway and Wall Street........................................ 191

CLOSING PRAYER........................................................................195

Review Request............................................................................197

About the Author...........................................................................199

Arise Women's Conference ..........................................................201

Author's Acknowledgments...........................................................203

# FOREWORD

I have loved Melodi from the moment I met her! I've loved having she and her husband Brandon as a part of Healing Place Church in Baton Rouge, Louisiana, where we were their pastors for years before they started I Heart Church in Beckley, West Virginia through the Association of Related Churches. I have watched her battle through difficult times, but she has never wavered and has always kept her smile and has continued to bless others in the midst of it all. She's an inspiration to me and has been an encouragement to my life. I'm so proud of her and how God is using her at their church, with women, and through this book.

Melodi, as you'll see in this devotional, is one of those people who has a contagious authenticity. She makes those who meet her want to be true to themselves. She is so beautifully confident in God's love for her that it makes the rest of us who are blessed to have been around her want to be more aware of God's love for us, too.

Her writing is no different from her life. It makes her a joy to be around, and I'm excited that this book will bring to so many others the chance to get to know her as well. But even more important, this book will give its readers a look at the magnificent love that Jesus has for all of us in a very practical and life-changing way.

Melodi's deep devotion to Jesus in her own private life is a great strength of this book. In a sense, she is sharing the personal relationship she has with Jesus with the rest of us, and I know it will be a tremendous blessing to you as it has been to me.

I hope and pray that as you read this book you will find yourself challenged to draw closer to Jesus, to believe and trust Him more, to love Him more, and to believe in His love for you like never before.

I pray that you will find yourself doing what this book is all about: Awake, Arise, and Shine!

—DeLynn Rizzo, ARC Women Association of Related Churches, Birmingham, Alabama

# AWAKE, ARISE, & SHINE

Forty days. It's a significant time frame in Scripture. Moses was on the mountain for forty days and forty nights when he received the Ten Commandments (on two separate occasions in both Exodus 24:18 and 34:1–28). The prophet Elijah fasted for forty days at Mount Horeb. Jesus fasted for forty days in the wilderness before entering into His ministry. Many biblical scholars agree that the number forty represents a time of testing or trial.

I myself have been on a few life-changing forty-day journeys. Nudged by a still, small voice, I experienced these meaningful times in my life when I felt prompted to "get away and draw nearer" to my heavenly Father. Most often, on these forty-day journeys, I coupled fasting (from certain foods or activities) with an increase in personal time with God. For instance, I would replace social media or television with a new Christian devotional or sermon podcast series in addition to my normal Bible reading and prayer time. These intense forty-day journeys were designed to be a "spiritual detox," if you will, to help whip me into shape. They quieted the voices around me so that I could increase my intimacy with God. These times in my life proved to be monumental. Some of the biggest spiritual and emotional breakthroughs I have ever experienced resulted from these decisions to dedicate forty days to seeking the heart of God like never before.

Inspired by the beauty of what these "soul detoxes" have achieved in my own Christian walk, I desired to create a forty-day devotional journey for women who, like me, feel the quiet whisper of Jesus to "draw near."

The next forty days of our ARISE Journey will be divided into three phases. The end of each day's devotion will include an "action step" designed to put what we have learned into practice. The three ARISE Journey phases are as follows:

## The AWAKEN Phase

This is the starting point, where we will have a time of deep introspection. Much of this section is dedicated to jolting us out of wrong thought patterns and "waking us up" from a spiritual stupor or fog. This will be a time of deep self-examination of underlying emotional, mental, and spiritual stumbling blocks that keep us from living victoriously. This phase is all about the mind and heart. What lies from the enemy have we believed that are causing us to stumble or walk in pain? What mental decisions do we need to make in order to experience true freedom?

## The ARISE Phase

The second part of our journey will include practical steps to begin getting up from destructive lifestyle patterns. If you have ever been guilty of hitting the snooze button and yelling, "I'm awake, I'm awake!" in an effort to stay in bed longer, you know that being awake simply isn't enough! We must rise up and begin to take action. Using God's Word as a guide, we will "get up and walk out" what we have learned from the Awaken Phase through practical, yet challenging biblical mandates.

## The SHINE Phase

During the final part of our journey, we will shift from receiving personal victory over bondage to experiencing empowerment to use our journeys for eternal purposes. God awakens us for a purpose: to shine as a beacon of hope for others who are hurting. Our focus will change during this last stage to one of "others-ness," in which we will see that we were meant to live for more than just ourselves, and that God has a job for us to do while we are here on the earth. It is in this final stage that we will begin to find the joy that results from living our lives with an eternal Kingdom perspective.

I am so thrilled that you are taking this journey with me. Before we begin, please take time to pray and ask God whether you should abstain (or, fast) from any activities or foods, and replace them with more time spent in worship, prayer, and Bible study. Remember—you will get out of this journey what you put into it. Don't be afraid to go all-in! I also encourage you to grab a journal in order to document what God speaks to your heart, list your prayers and concerns, and chart your spiritual progress along the way.

I hope you are ready. We are about to go on a 40-day ARISE Journey, and I can't wait to see what God will do!

Congratulations on beginning your journey!

Take time to watch a special message from the author before beginning by visiting arisejourney.com/beforeyoubegin.

# VISION DAY

## DAY 1.
## Clumsy Like Me

*And taking the child by the hand, He said to her, "Talitha kum!"*
*[which translated means, Little girl, I say to you, arise!].*
*And immediately the girl rose and began to walk.*
Mark 5:41–42 (NASB)

I have always been a bit clumsy. As a child, I remember frequently bumping into things and constantly having bruised knees and a broken ego. On top of this, I was NOT a particularly *cute* girl. I was one of five sisters, so (for fiscal reasons) my mom would cut our hair at home. This inevitably left me with a mullet. Pair the mullet with a big space between my two front teeth, and then add in a smidge of pudginess and an extra dose of clumsiness and *this was ME*. Clumsy Mel.

I didn't notice how awkward I was until high school. Of course, if you have ANY flaws whatsoever, high school will sift them out faster than water being strained from spaghetti noodles.

I remember being so anxious to prove myself in high school that I once obliviously face-planted into a huge white column in our high school's commons area.

BAM. (I think it left a mark.)

But one particularly horrific memory of clumsiness left me almost scarred for life. I still cringe to think about it.

It was my first-ever high school football game. (I was a freshman.) I got dolled up and met a few friends at the game. The cute high school boys always sat in the front, bottom section of the bleachers at the home games. Obviously, if you wanted to sit *anywhere* in the bleachers, you had to walk by *them*.

Those boys were loud and opinionated. I just wanted to walk by without being seen, for fear that Clumsy Mel would say or do something to ruin my fresh, new, volatile ninth-grade social image. So, before the game began, I mustered up all the courage I had and prepared to walk past the boys to find my seat *(with my friends, of course, because high school girls don't go anywhere alone)*. After concentrating hard while walking across, *"Whew!"* I made it! Clumsy, awkward Mel sat down in confidence, completely proud of herself.

But about twenty minutes later, the group of girls I was with became restless and decided to go to the bathroom as a tribe. (They would go on to do this every twenty minutes or so for the remainder of the game.) I couldn't possibly stay there in the bleachers alone, so I followed along. But, of course, we would again have to walk past the section of boys.

This time, I was feeling a bit more confident. So I tried to walk down the bleachers WHILE TALKING to my friends (so as to deflect from my nervousness).

Let me stop here for just a moment.

Okay, so you may be insightful enough to see where this is headed. Hindsight teaches me at least two things:

> 1. Clumsy girls shouldn't try to walk and talk at the same time.

> 2. Going DOWN the bleachers is much harder than walking UP them.

But young, awkward, mullet-Melodi didn't know these things until it was too late. Yep, down she went! Thumping and falling down the bleachers, landing at the feet of the laughing, cute older boys. I wanted these boys to notice me. *But not like this!*

I composed myself as best as I could, consoled by my fellow freshmen girlfriends, and then proceeded to the bathroom, *where I cried.* For the remainder of the night, every time my squad would pass by the older boys, one of them would yell out, "Hey! Isn't THAT the girl who fell?!"

Ouch. It hurt. And, honestly, I still can't walk down a set of bleachers without carefully considering each step and glancing around for mean, older boys.

It hurts to fall.

Spiritually, I've been clumsy, too. Although I came to know Jesus at a young age, my journey has been marked by bruised shins and bloodied knees. I've made too many personal failures to count. Mistakes I'm not proud of. Mistakes that sometimes heckle me like mean high school boys. Mistakes that have even left me wondering, *What's the point in getting back up?*

At my lowest point, I even remember wondering if life was worth living, asking God whether the world would be better off without stupid, failing Clumsy Mel.

You may be in a similar situation as you read this. Maybe you're at a low point, on the ground at the feet of taunting observers. Maybe you have received a sentence of death in a situation or circumstance and you're asking yourself, "How can I possibly get up from this?"

If you look through the pages of Scripture, you'll find no shortage of clumsy women. Jesus loved them. He was drawn to pursue them, going out of His sacred way to find them: at lonely wells *(cue the Samaritan woman)*, being sentenced to death *(cue the adulteress woman)*, or working when they should be resting *(cue Martha, Martha)*. Jesus always LOVED His clumsy, messy girls.

But there's one particular passage of Scripture that has altered my life. It's found in Mark 5. Jesus had been called to go to the house of a man named Jairus to heal his dying daughter. But before Jesus could get there, Jairus's twelve-year-old girl passed away. Because of the finality of death (well, generally speaking, that is), the messengers tried to discourage Jairus from even bringing Jesus back to his house.

Let's start reading here, in verse 36:

> *But Jesus, overhearing what was being spoken, said to the synagogue official (Jairus), "Do not be afraid any longer, only believe." And He allowed no one to accompany Him, except Peter and James and John the brother of James. They came to the house of the synagogue official; and He saw a commotion, and people loudly weeping and wailing. And entering in, He said to them, "Why make a commotion and weep? The child has not died, but is asleep." They began laughing at Him. But putting them all out, He took along the child's father and mother and His own companions, and entered the room where the child was. Taking the child by the hand, He said to her, "Talitha kum!" (which translated means, "Little girl, I say to you, get up!"). Immediately the girl got up and began to walk.* Mark 5:36–42a (NASB)

What a story! I love how differently Jesus sees things than people do. Discontented with the crowd's conclusions (no matter how rational they were), Jesus made His own conclusion to the end of this girl's story! What others saw as dead, He saw as merely asleep. So He sounded His holy alarm and brought back to life what had been impossibly dead. With one little phrase (*"Girl, I say to you, ARISE!"*), He inked in a comma where others had placed a definitive period.

Today, I'm not sure what your situation looks like. Maybe you are clumsy like me... Maybe you are face-down on the dirty bleachers with the taunts of the enemy reminding you how final your situation seems to be. Maybe you're not even sure if you want to get up. I have been there. But I believe that if you can look up with spiritual eyes, you will see the loving, nail-scarred hand of the Savior, reaching out for you. If you will listen, you will hear the voice of the One who spoke the universe into existence, saying, "Girl, I say to you, ARISE."

My prayer for you as we begin our ARISE Journey is that you may encounter *this Jesus* along the way. This Jesus who makes messy, clumsy, broken, bruised misfits into beautiful creatures in His image. May you see yourself as He sees you. May you feel Him reach out for you right now as you read these words. And may hope arise in your heart, the understanding that you can get up from anything when Jesus is calling your name—even if you're clumsy like me.

## TODAY'S ACTION STEP

As we begin our 40-day ARISE Journey, take time to write down in a journal some things that you want to get out of this experience. Are there any situations that you feel are hopeless in your life? What are you believing for or asking God to do in you during this time? (Some examples might include: *I want God to heal me from bitterness and resentment. I want God to break my addiction to lust, prescription pills, overeating, or nicotine. I want to have the courage to sever destructive relationships. I want to be freed from the shame of my past. I want God to heal my marriage.*)

After you have written down your goals for this journey, take time to talk to God and tell Him the desires of your heart. Ask Him to increase your faith to believe that He is able to do a miraculous work in any situation that you face.

*ARISE! by Melodi Hawley*

# THE AWAKEN PHASE

*Awake, sleeper, and arise from the dead,*
*And Christ will shine on you.*
Ephesians 5:14 (NASB)

The Awaken Phase is the starting point of our journey, where we will spend some time in deep soul-searching. Much of this section is dedicated to jolting us out of wrong thought patterns for the purpose of "waking us up" from a spiritual stupor or fog. This will be a time of intense self-examination of underlying emotional, mental, and spiritual stumbling blocks that keep us from living victoriously. This phase is all about the mind and the heart.

# DAY 2.
# Spilled Milk, Broken Lives

*Our lives are like water spilled out on the ground, which cannot be gathered up again. But God does not just sweep life away; instead he devises ways to bring us back when we have been separated from him.*
2 Samuel 14:14 (NLT)

It's hard not to cry over spilled milk. Especially when that milk is all we have ever known. A marriage ends. A loved one dies. A hope is shattered.

It's heart-wrenching to stand back and watch as pieces of our lives fall apart at the seams, or our dreams begin to slip through our fingers. It's easy to sit back and wonder where God is in all of the mess. Has He forgotten me? Have I caused this?

Girl, have I been there! The darkest moments of my life were those times when I looked around and realized I had made a mess of something God had given me, and it was too late to fix it.

This was an irreconcilable spill. Bottom line: You can't put the spilt milk back in the cup.

And how do you NOT cry about that? How do you just get up and move on when all you can see is the destruction of your marriage, your finances, your dreams, or your kids, broken in the wake of YOUR mistakes?

Being in full-time ministry, I have not only seen some extremely broken situations, but I have been a victim of them myself. Yes, I have personally experienced the ugly side of life that no one talks about. The dark side. I have had moments of heaviness, brokenness, and bitterness, moments of shame, humiliation, and utter hopelessness, moments of my own personal depravity. Many of those moments stemmed from my own selfish choices. And if I can be transparent with you, I have even had moments of wanting to die, just to escape the consequences of those choices.

What a dark place, this place of "spilled milk."

It was precisely in one of those dark moments when I stumbled upon this short, obscure verse in 2 Samuel 14:14 (NLT): "*Our lives are like water spilled out on the ground, which cannot be gathered up again. But God does not just sweep life away; instead he devises ways to bring us back when we have been separated from him.*"

Wow. God can not only "clean up the mess," but He can even put it back into the cup! As a matter of fact, He loves us so much that He will strategically design ways to use our messes to bring us home again. I know He did this for me.

The word in the Hebrew here for "devises" can be translated as "plait, weave, fabricate, plot, compute." This tells us that God is, right now, computing a way, plotting a path, weaving a plan for your redemption! I believe this journey is a part of that "plot" for your homecoming. He divinely orchestrates just the right pieces at just the right times so that He can restore you to Himself.

Perhaps today you are looking at your spilled cup. Let me assure you, no matter how desperate or dark the situation you are in may seem, God can heal it. He does not just sweep you away. He is not afraid of your mess. He does not brush your life under some rug. He does not look away from you. He is, right now, devising a way to bring you back to Him to restore your hope.

I can honestly say that today my cup has not only been gathered back up, but it is overflowing. And when I look back at those darkest of moments, I love Him even more for bringing me through them.

So, before you give up, look up. There is One who is waiting to love you in the midst of your mess. He is waiting to bring you home again.

## TODAY'S ACTION STEP

Early in our journey, my prayer is that faith will rise up in your heart to see the possibility of the total transformation of your life. I pray that you will see that God CAN INDEED redeem any part of your broken life, through your obedience to His Word and by His Spirit. Rest assured, this will be a difficult journey. He will ask you to align your plans with His, but His is a plan you can trust. Right now, commit to giving God your complete devotion during this journey. Ask Him for the faith to believe that you can and will see restoration, healing, and freedom.

*ARISE! by Melodi Hawley*

# DAY 3.
# Junkyard Valley

*I will return her vineyards to her and transform the Valley of Trouble into a gateway of hope.*
Hosea 2:15 (NLT)

I was raised in South Louisiana, so I am accustomed to flatlands and swamps. My husband, Brandon, however, is from the hills of West Virginia. When he first moved to Louisiana (where we met), he would jokingly refer to it as the "armpit of America." I was offended! This swampy, below-sea-level landscape had a certain sentimental beauty to me.

And then, he took me to his hometown in West Virginia. And while I still don't let him call Louisiana an "armpit," I can definitely see why someone raised in those beautiful mountains would have trouble adjusting to such a contrasting landscape! Seriously, you can absolutely empathize with John Denver when he sang that West Virginia is "almost heaven."

Although it's been several years since we moved to West Virginia, this Cajun girl still regularly finds herself in a "trance" as we drive through these country roads. I often observe the landscape in complete wonder, just trying to take in the amazing scenery.

One particular memory sticks out to me from the early days of our move to West Virginia. It was several years ago, and we were driving back from North Carolina. I was caught up in my trancelike state. As was typical for me on long, winding mountain-road trips,

I was going back and forth between sheer panic, thinking we were about to drive off of a cliff, and being in awe of the view. When I wasn't hyperventilating from fear, I was taking it all in, noticing the enormous mountain peaks and the deep valleys. Wow! It was amazing. There is something about the grandeur of the mountains that stands out even more when you can see how far the valleys dip down.

But as we drove past one area, I noticed a particular valley that, while it had a breathtaking view, was also occupied by a junkyard. Here, in the worst possible place, was a yard filled with junk cars and trash! *How could the owners let that happen? Don't they realize what a beautiful piece of land they own? Who in their right mind would fill such a piece of heaven with busted-up Ford Tempos??!! It should be against the law!*

And then I had another thought: God did not create our valleys to be filled with our junk, *either.* He created our valleys to display His glory even more when we are on the mountaintop. I thought about Joseph: Talk about a man who had been through some deep valleys! His life's troubles would put most of ours to shame! And yet, the beauty of his story was not in Joseph's rise to success. What causes us to be so inspired by Joseph's life is his response to profound pain. We still marvel at his forgiveness, grace, and integrity despite the enormous betrayal and heartbreaking injustices he experienced.

I cry every time I read the end of Joseph's story, as he turned his head to weep when he met his brothers face-to-face, only to end up loving and saving them from starvation (see Genesis 42 and Genesis 50:16–21). Here, in this epic story, what makes his "mountaintop" success so beautiful is the contrast of the deep valley he had come out of. This was where we learned that God delights in using what the enemy means for our destruction for the "saving of many."

But what if Joseph had not lived with such integrity and grace in his valley? What if he had fought back, ladder-climbed, sought out his personal rights, posted rants on Facebook *(okay, I know he didn't have Facebook, but you get the drift)*, or told everyone and their mama all of the bad things that had been done to him? What if he had worn his wounds like badges to earn sympathy? What if he had preferred the stench of the prison to the aroma of compassion? He would have filled his beautiful valley with junk.

I meet so many people who cannot realize that their valley is actually a beautiful place. They miss that God has allowed this deep chasm of pain to provide a place of intimacy and brokenness that will be breathtaking when looking from the mountaintop. Instead of walking through their valley with grace, they fill it up with drama, drama, drama.

How tragic it is when we pollute such a God-ordained season with our junk! When we do this, we essentially negate God from getting glory from our hurt.

Today, if you are in a valley, take time to look around. You will not always be here. How you respond to this season will affect both you and others when you come out of it. Let me encourage you to handle it with grace by depending on God each day and trusting in Him to use this season for His glory and for your eventual good. Trust Him to walk with you through this valley and redeem every tear wept here for His purpose. Take time to ask yourself, *When I am on the mountaintop, will I regret how I have chosen to walk through this valley?* Determine to make your pain count by allowing God to create something beautiful out of it. You'll be so glad you did.

## TODAY'S ACTION STEP

Be honest with yourself. How have you handled your "valley seasons?" Do you have any regrets? Does it change your response to pain to know that others (i.e., your children, your family members, unbelievers) may find Christ through your proper response to hurt?

Today, take time to pray and ask God to identify any "junk" in your heart that may be polluting your season. Ask God to renew your mind (your thinking) with His Word and with the promise that even difficult seasons are temporary. Remember that He will work everything out for your "eventual good" if you allow Him to use them. If you have never done so before, try to carve out time over the next few days to read Joseph's story (Genesis 37–50) and write down his responses to the injustices he faced. How can Joseph's story inspire you to do better?

# DAY 4.
# The Vacant Room Down the Hall

*For the Lord will comfort Zion. He will comfort all her waste places. He will make her desert like Eden, like the garden of the Lord. Joy and happiness will be found in her. There will be much giving of thanks and much singing.*
Isaiah 51:3 (NLT)

Several years ago, while traveling during Christmastime, we received an invitation to stay with a very dear friend of mine from Bible college. It had been nine years since we had last seen one another face-to-face, so I was elated at the chance to finally get to see her again. I could not wait to take a stroll down memory lane with her, to reminisce about the "good ol' days" and to find out all about what God was doing in her life. Ours is a type of relationship that could go ten years without communicating and suddenly pick back up right where we had left off. She was and is a true friend.

When we arrived at her house, she had a beautiful meal prepared for us. She insisted on sleeping on the couch so that we could have her room. That's just the kind of person she is. After dinner, I walked up the stairs to her hallway and put my things down in her room. When I came out, I glanced around the rest of the upstairs, eager to see the décor in her adorable little townhouse. As I peeked around, admiring her personality reflected in each room, I finally came to the only room left I hadn't yet explored.

When I opened the door, my heart broke. Here was a room perfectly decorated to welcome a baby boy. Adorned with soft blues and browns, a sign that scrolled across the wall read: *"For this child I prayed"* (1 Samuel 1:27, ESV). One year's supply of diapers was even stacked neatly on the floor. The only thing missing was—the baby.

My friend and her husband had been trying to conceive to no avail for three years. After extensive medical treatments, they finally began exploring the possibility of adoption. And then, a miracle happened! A young pregnant girl decided she would place her son with my friend and her husband, much to their excitement. As the young mom's due date approached, my friend prepared the room down the hall in eager anticipation of the day when God would finally answer her prayers for a child. Everything seemed to fall into place perfectly, from the finances to the paperwork. They watched in amazement as God seemed to smile down on them with favor through the entire process. When the baby was born, however, things changed. At the last moment, the young mother changed her mind.

Two months later, there sat a vacant room down the hall.

As we talked that night, I listened to her story. When I looked into her eyes, the joy of naïveté and youth that I remembered from nine years ago was gone. Instead, her eyes were full of pain, hurt, brokenness, and discouragement. Perhaps most difficult of all was the lack of care and understanding demonstrated by those around her. Most could not see the silent suffering she was enduring. My heart broke for her as I saw the same vacancy in her eyes as had been present in that room down the hall.

Truth be told, we all have "vacant rooms down the hall"—hollow places of pain and shattered dreams that we prefer to keep locked up so that we are not reminded of the brokenness they represent. These are the rooms inside each of us that we weren't prepared for as children in Sunday school. These are the "wasted places" in our lives that are formed when we are left feeling abandoned. Although we pray, believe, seek God, and do all we know to do, these vacant rooms still sit as a reminder of the emptiness left when we begin to believe we have misunderstood God or failed to hear Him at all.

The Christian community doesn't often acknowledge these vacant rooms. It's awkward to talk about. Uncomfortable. Even faithless. You never hear someone giving a testimony in church about how God did NOT answer a prayer. But the longer I'm around in this world, the more I realize that just about everyone has shattered, broken dreams, these vacant waste places that sit as memorials of what "should have been."

Frankly, for me, my "vacant room" was the second trimester miscarriage I had in 2010. My husband and I have been through some pretty tough times, mind you, and we have weathered a lot of storms through God's grace. I have had two other miscarriages and nearly lost my middle daughter on several occasions to sickness. We have suffered job loss, isolation, and rejection; we have been falsely accused, hurt, and maligned. Yet none of those things seemed to affect me quite like the time when I lost that baby.

I can very honestly, and with raw emotion, say that it was a near breaking point for me—mostly because it seemed so contrary to everything I believed I had heard God speak. It would take me hours to recount all the Scriptures I had journaled during that time, how many "words" I had received, how much confirmation I had that, no matter what the doctors were saying, this baby would live and not die.

But despite all those things—my child did die.

I had dealt with death before. It was not death I could not take. It was the possibility that I did not know my Savior's voice. It was the whispers that told me I could not depend on my ability to hear from Him. Why was I not ready for this? If *"the Lord confides in those who fear Him"* (Psalm 25:14, NIV), why did He not prepare me for this ending? Where were all the Scriptures I had held on to in the finality of this baby's death?

Some of those questions, I still don't have answers for. But there is one thing I do know: As I chose to worship Him in the midst of that pain, as I chose to sing when my heart wanted to wail, as I denied myself the right to think that I somehow knew better than God, and the more I forced myself to confess that my God was a GOOD God who loved me and had a good plan for my life, and as I released my broken heart—I met God in a way I never had before. I discovered that, although He does not work in OUR ways, or in OUR time, or inside of OUR realm of understanding, He *is* a God who will come running to meet us in the midst of whatever pain He has called us to walk through.

That empty, vacant room down the hall is the place that God has allowed to be vacant in order to fill it with Himself. The pain of it keeps many of us from ever opening the door again. But if we will open it up, walk in, fall at His feet, and cry out to Him, right smack in the middle of our hurt and pain, He will fill that vacant room with such a lavish grace and a knowledge of Himself that we will want for little else. And even when those dreams are finally a reality and not a disappointment, you wouldn't ever trade that bittersweet experience with Jesus for anything.

Isaiah 51:3 (NLT) says, *"For the Lord will comfort Zion. He will comfort all her waste places."*

Do you have a "wasted place" or a vacant room in your life? Today, the God of all comfort is waiting for you there. He stands behind the door of that room, not intimidated by your questions and uncertainty. He desires to bring joy to even the darkest corners of your heart. Friend, God can and will take that room and transform it into an altar of worship and a place of healing, if you'll only have the courage to let Him. You see, that sacred, vacant room always was, and always will be, HIS to fill.

## TODAY'S ACTION STEP

As you read the story of the vacant room, do any painful, unanswered questions come to mind? Do you have any tragic or confusing experiences in your past that may not be completely resolved in your heart? How does it make you feel to know that God is not intimidated or deterred by our difficult questions?

Today, take out your journal and begin to write any questions you may have for the Lord. You may even want to write down your own painful story, as a release. When you are finished, play a worship song and begin to confess the goodness of God even in the midst of your pain. Instead of trying to "shut the door" on those painful experiences, take time to acknowledge them and worship God through them.

Remember that He promises: *"He will make her deserts like Eden, her wastelands like the garden of the LORD. Joy and gladness will be found in her, thanksgiving and the sound of singing"* (Isaiah 51:3, NIV).

# DAY 5.
# Baby Fingers

*Search me, O God, and know my heart; test me and know my
anxious thoughts. Point out anything in me that offends you, and
lead me along the path of everlasting life.*
Psalm 139:23–24 (NLT)

On July 5, 2004, I became a mom. I was young—just twenty-one
years old—but it was easily one of the most miraculous moments
of my life. I remember time seemingly standing still as I watched
this barely six-pound, curly blonde-haired baby girl make her
grand entrance into the world. Everything else in my life dimmed
in the light of my almost obsessive love for her.

In the days that followed, I found it hard to concentrate on
anything else but my new daughter. She amazed me. Everything
she did was delightful (she even earned congratulating cheers for
filling her diaper). I would take upwards of two hundred pictures
of her each day. (No kidding, I told you I was obsessed!)

When she nursed or slept, I would examine her tiny body, in a
mixture of awe and concern. Beginning with her tiny baby fingers,
I would make sure each part of her was healthy. During one such
examination, I remember finding a little patchwork of purple
birthmarks on the nape of her neck. I promptly called our
pediatrician. Of course, it was normal. This was just how God had
uniquely "marked" her—His creative tattoo.

You may think my parental love is over the top or even strange.
But let me assure you, the kind of love God has for you is even

*more* intense! Like a new mother, He obsesses over you! He delights in you! Don't believe me? Check out these passages from Psalm 139 (NLT):

> *O Lord, you have examined my heart*
> *and know everything about me.*
> *You know when I sit down or stand up.*
> *You know my thoughts even when I'm far away.*
> *You see me when I travel*
> *and when I rest at home.*
> *You know everything I do.*
> *You know what I am going to say*
> *even before I say it, Lord.*
> *You go before me and follow me.*
> *You place Your hand of blessing on my head.*
> *Such knowledge is too wonderful for me,*
> *too great for me to understand! (verses 1-6)*

> *You watched me as I was being formed in utter seclusion,*
> *as I was woven together in the dark of the womb.*
> *You saw me before I was born.*
> *Every day of my life was recorded in your book.*
> *Every moment was laid out*
> *before a single day had passed.*
> *How precious are your thoughts about me, O God.*
> *They cannot be numbered!*
> *I can't even count them;*
> *they outnumber the grains of sand!*
> *And when I wake up,*
> *you are still with me! (verses 15–18)*

What a thought! The God of the universe cares about every detail of His baby girl! (That's *you!*)

But I want to take this train of thought a little further: My oldest daughter is now a teenager. Can you imagine if I were to examine her big girl fingers or celebrate her trips to the bathroom like I did when she was a newborn? Although I still desire to know her intimately and be deeply involved in her life, the dynamics of our relationship have inevitably changed!

She and I have a beautiful bond. I still actively pursue her heart, pray for her, and desire great involvement in her life. I continue to emotionally and spiritually "search her" and "examine her" to know and keep her heart. However, the major difference is that now this "knowing" is done with her permission. It is by invitation only. I cannot force myself into the recesses of her heart. She can choose to shut me out, close me off, or push me away. And love is what gives her that choice.

It is impossible to miss the Father's deep, obsessive love in the early verses of Psalm 139. Yet in the end of this chapter (verses 23–24, NIV), you can see the psalmist's response to that love: *"Search me, O God, and know my heart; test me and know my anxious thoughts. Point out anything in me that offends you and lead me along the path of everlasting life."* He willingly invites God to continue to search him and know him. He offers his heart to be read like an open book to the only One with the power to find hidden faults that no one else sees. He vulnerably asks his Father to continue the examination, to expose any inner motives— anything that could keep him from the way everlasting.

As we mature and grow in our faith, we, too, will be afforded this opportunity, a chance to invite God to continually inspect our hearts and to know us. Like a loving, patient Father, He won't cross boundaries where He's not wanted. He leaves the option on the table with a simple love note: *"Will you let Me in?"*

Today, I pray you will find comfort in knowing that God deeply desires intimacy with you. I challenge you to trust Him with your whole heart and allow Him to thoroughly examine your motives, your heart, and your life so that He can heal you and lead you in the everlasting way.

## TODAY'S ACTION STEP

Read Psalm 139 and highlight the portions that mean the most to you. How does it feel to know that you are God's baby girl? He is wild about you! Yet, what is your response to that extravagant love? Do you allow Him complete access to your life, heart, and inner motives?

Take time to ask God to search you and know you, to point out anything in your heart that may be hindering your relationship with Him. Write down anything He reveals to you during this time of prayer and reflection.

# DAY 6.
# This Old House

*You will rebuild the deserted ruins of your cities. Then you will be known as a rebuilder of walls and a restorer of homes.*
Isaiah 58:12 (NLT)

Four years ago (after eleven years of marriage), my husband and I bought our first home. It was in no way what I pictured we would ultimately call our first place. This old house was new to us, but it was actually 110 years old!

To be honest, my reaction to the house when we first viewed it from the outside wasn't a pleasant one. We pulled in the driveway, and I was already on my phone looking at other homes. I had written this one off before we ever took a step inside! The neighborhood around the home looked outdated and old. I wasn't impressed with the abandoned buildings and lack of "subdivision-type" curb appeal.

But then I walked inside…

The family who had purchased the home before us (just a few years before) had stripped this old house down and rebuilt it to code. They restored a see-through (middle-of-the-room) stone fireplace they found hidden inside a wall. They put on a new roof; installed new plumbing; set in place new windows; put in heating and air-conditioning systems; installed custom cabinetry, granite countertops, and recessed lighting through the entire house; and even built a new foundation. My mouth nearly dropped to the floor when I walked in, and it was love at first sight. I loved the character of the home combined with the modern updates; I was SOLD!

God worked out an amazing deal, and we moved in and made it our own.

In the weeks leading up to us moving in, I couldn't shake the thought that this house was somehow like my life. This house and I shared a bond that I couldn't ignore.

I imagined what it must have looked like prior to its renovation. I thought often about how much easier it would have been for the previous owners to just tear down the old house, worn out by years of abuse and neglect. And yet somehow, someone saw the beauty of what it could be and trudged through the work to restore this home into something beautiful again.

Much like Jesus did with me.

I'm reminded every time I look at that stone fireplace (once dilapidated and forgotten inside a wall) of verses like Isaiah 61:3 (NLT): *"To all who mourn in Israel, he will give a crown of beauty for ashes, a joyous blessing instead of mourning, festive praise instead of despair."*

I think of myself at my lowest. In the depravity of my mistakes. In the heartache of my own personal failures. I think about the hidden potential God saw cocooned in a life of misery, loss, and sin. My mind flashes back to the nights when I was so far away from God that I felt I had no real reason to live. That I was too far-gone to be forgiven. I also remember the night when God wooed my heart. How He spoke tenderly to me that He could undo the mess I had made, if I would only let Him.

Thank goodness for a Savior who is not frightened off by our broken condition! Instead, He DELIGHTS in finding hidden treasures in the least likely of places. He is the Master Restorer, and no "old house" is too difficult, too far gone, or too messed up for Him to create a masterpiece out of it!

Christ is not like us. He does not have to see the finished product to fall in love at first sight. He is in love with you right now, right where you are. And do you want to know the best part about God's renovations? He does not restore us to what we WERE, but to what we were INTENDED TO BE!

Today, I don't care how far you think you are in the muck and the mire, Jesus Christ can pull you out! I don't know what kind of mess you have found yourself in, but I know what kind of Master Builder we serve. He is at the door of your heart right now, waiting for you to allow Him to begin sweeping away the dust and rebuilding your broken life to make it into something beautiful again.

## TODAY'S ACTION STEP

Write down your answers to the following questions:

What is your response to the idea that God sees hidden potential in you that (perhaps) even you can't see? What if, like that old fireplace buried inside a wall, you are housing something rare and beautiful that the world needs? Do you feel there are areas of your life or past that disqualify you from God using you in a major way? Do you feel too far-gone for God's restoration?

Take time to write down some areas that you would like to see renovated by the hand of God. Ask the Father to continue to restore you during this journey and to give you faith to believe that nothing is too broken, when He is your homebuilder.

# DAY 7.
# I Want an Orange Nose

*He was not aware that his face was radiant because he had spoken with the Lord.*
Exodus 34:29b (NIV)

I want an orange nose. You read that right. I want an ORANGE NOSE. Okay, maybe I just said that to spark your curiosity, because I don't *literally* want an orange nose. But *symbolically*, I want my nose to look like it fell into a can of spray tan!

If you were to take a glimpse through my super-organized photo albums *(okay, I admit...there aren't any albums; most of my pictures are still in my phone),* you would notice a strange, familiar thread. Around the age of eight months, all four of my children share the same orange nose. If you are a mom, you may know what causes it: too much beta-carotene from eating lots of carrots, sweet potatoes, and other orange veggies.

Many baby books call it the "healthy orange glow," and my babies' faces lit up like big, orange light bulbs! It may look peculiar, but it is actually a sign of good health. Their faces showed what they had been eating. They could not hide it.

Moses didn't glow orange, but his face lit up, too, for an entirely different reason. Exodus 34:29 (NIV) says, *"When Moses came down from Mount Sinai with the two tablets of the covenant law in his hands, he was not aware that his face was radiant because he had spoken with the Lord."*

Friend, what you do in private eventually surfaces. What you take in, read, and watch; who you spend time with—it all eventually shows up in how you shine or not. Like Moses, you may not even be able to tell that you are radiant, but others most assuredly will.

Recently, one of my children who had never had a cavity in her life came home from the dentist with not one, but SIX cavities! I was disturbed. We help her brush her teeth regularly and limit her sugar intake, so how in the world could she have so many (sudden) cavities? The doctor said she had "enamel hypoplasia," which takes place when the adult teeth come in with little or no enamel to protect them. The cause is usually some type of malnutrition during the first year of life, when the adult teeth are forming.

This particular child, although she had eaten lots of veggies, had also had terrible acid reflux and could barely keep her food down. She was classified as "failure to thrive" on many occasions during that first year of her life. The effects of that malnutrition are surfacing even years later.

I'm making a point here: *Your spiritual diet matters.* What you take in *and absorb* matters! It's not enough to read God's Word, only to vomit it back up before true digestion and application can happen. We don't spend time in God's presence to check off some sort of godly to-do list. The Bible is clear that we are to be DOERS of the Word, not just hearers (See James 1:22). We have to eat, ingest, <u>and process</u> God's Word in our lives so that it comes out of every fiber of our being.

What good is it to read and take in God's Word if we do not keep it down long enough to let it change us? If we are not living out what we are reading, then that, too, will manifest itself. Our healthy, spiritual growth will be stunted; we will begin to rot because we are starving the inner man, who is designed to grow on God's Word.

In ministry, I see so many people who have been raised in church, and yet they still act like babies. One thing I notice happening often is new Christians (saved for only a couple of years) surpassing those who have been saved for twenty-plus years. This happens because the new Christian has an insatiable hunger for God, while the older Christian is stagnant and starving. Equally sad is the fact that usually those older Christians are the only ones who cannot tell that they have lost their glow and are dying of spiritual malnutrition. Rotting and decaying instead of shining and thriving.

The last time I checked, you don't have to coach a child to grow. I have never had to look at my babies and plead, *"Grow, child! GROW! For all that is good in the world, baby, please grow!"* Growing is a natural by-product of health. If a child is eating and absorbing her food properly, she will grow on her own.

Christians should not need constant coaching, pleading, begging, five-step growth seminars, family member or friend interventions, or spiritual feeding tubes. If you are a healthy Christian, spending time in God's Word and applying it to your life, you will grow naturally. The life and beauty of God's Word will manifest itself in the fruit that you bear. The result will be a life that shines.

So, what color is your nose? Are you still glowing? Have you lost that hunger for God's Word? (If you are really brave, ask those around you for honest feedback. Let them tell you whether or not you're glowing!)

The good news is this: *"Blessed are those who hunger and thirst for righteousness"* (Matthew 5:6, NIV).

This morning, take some time to pull up to God's table and grab a plate. Your Father is waiting to make you shine.

## TODAY'S ACTION STEP

Today, take a moment to think about how much time you spend in God's Word compared with the amount of time you spend on social media, watching television, or participating in other hobbies. Do you have an "orange nose"? Are you radiant from time spent in the Presence of Jesus? Have you seen an increase or a decrease in your hunger for God over the past several months? Look back through your journal. Go back over the verses you may have highlighted recently in your devotional or Bible. Are there any specific scriptures God has spoken to you that you have not fully absorbed? Write those down and commit to reading them over and over to yourself this week.

# DAY 8.
# Throwing Ants at Boys

*For the word of God is living and active, sharper than any two-edged sword, piercing to the division of soul and of spirit, of joints and of marrow, and discerning the thoughts and intentions of the heart.*
Hebrews 4:12 (ESV)

I was a spunky little girl. I was loud, bossy, and feisty.

Growing up, I led a neighborhood club for the kids on my block. I'm not sure why anyone wanted to be in *Lil' Melodi's Club*; I think it was more of a dictatorship. Each day, in order to participate in my club activities, you had to receive a new password from me. You could only do what I wanted you to do during club hours. If you offended me, I simply would not give you the next day's new password! *Wowzah!*

To further ensure my tyrannical reign, I learned a cruel scare tactic designed to ward off any boys who would try to come into my club and threaten my dictatorship: *throwing ants.* You read that right. *Throwing ants.*

Somewhere along the way, I figured out that if you take a handful of ants from an anthill and throw them at someone, the ants would sting the person they landed on, but they wouldn't have time to sting you yourself. (It works! But don't try this at home.) Boys would run screaming from my yard like a "bunch of little girls," and I could rule from my oppressive throne, unhindered.

Thankfully, I eventually outgrew throwing ants at boys. However, I do know others who still practice the art of "ant-slinging."

I think you can compare what I did as a "Stalin-ish" little girl to many Christians in the Church today, who sling Scriptures at anyone and everyone who offends them or who stands in their way. These ant-slingers use the Word of God as a weapon against others, rather than as a standard for their own lives. They hear a sermon and "amen" the pastor; they tweet quotes from Sunday's message; they repost scriptures and articles passive-aggressively aimed at others, all the while missing the fact that God's finger is pointed at their own hearts.

God's Word is a double-edged Sword, designed to pierce the deepest intentions of our hearts and minds in order to bring us true freedom. Yet many of us resist the sting of the Word and instead deflect from our own issues by using Scripture against others.

The Pharisees did this. In Matthew 23:2–5 (NLT) Jesus said, *"The teachers of religious law and the Pharisees are the official interpreters of the law of Moses. So practice and obey whatever they tell you, but don't follow their example. For they don't practice what they teach. They crush people with unbearable religious demands and never lift a finger to ease the burden. Everything they do is for show. On their arms they wear extra wide prayer boxes with Scripture verses inside, and they wear robes with extra-long tassels."*

He goes on to say in verses 23–26 (NLT): *"What sorrow awaits you teachers of religious law and you Pharisees. Hypocrites! For you are careful to tithe even the tiniest income from your herb gardens, but you ignore the more important aspects of the law— justice, mercy, and faith. You should tithe, yes, but do not neglect the more important things. Blind guides! You strain your water so you won't accidentally swallow a gnat, but you swallow a camel.*

*"What sorrow awaits you teachers of religious law and you Pharisees. Hypocrites! For you are so careful to clean the outside of the cup and the dish, but inside you are filthy—full of greed and self-indulgence! You blind Pharisee! First wash the inside of the cup and the dish, and then the outside will become clean, too."*

If you think Jesus sounds angry in these passages, you are right! He repeatedly talks to the Pharisees in this way. Jesus resented the hypocritical religious spirit that takes the Word of God and slings it without ever holding on to it long enough to change the person within.

Let me hypothesize for a moment that we all have the same potential to turn into a Pharisee. When we repeatedly hear the Word of God and don't apply it to ourselves, we are in danger of becoming a Pharisee. When we sit through a message and think, "So-and-so *really* needs to hear this!", we are in danger of becoming a Pharisee! When we think we cannot learn from others or we begin to become easily bored spiritually, we are in danger of becoming a Pharisee. We must be humble enough to learn from the "least of these," quiet enough to hear when God is speaking to us, and awake enough to see our own issues.

Jesus said that we must first get the "plank" out of our own eyes before we are able to help anyone else get the "speck" out of theirs. The problem with operating in a Pharisee spirit is that often everyone around us can see our pride, except for the one who is staring at us back in the mirror.

May our eyes be open to our own faults! May we hold on to the Word of God long enough for it to change us into the image of Christ Jesus. There is nothing wrong with sharing truth with others. But Jesus said that we must first get the plank out of our own eye, and then we will see clearly to help others with theirs.

I challenge you today to take some personal time for reflection. Are you holding on to God's Word even if it stings? Or are you just slinging it at other people? May we live with eyes wide open to see who we *really* are! I pray we can hold on to the often painful but always life-changing Word of God long enough to conform our own hearts into the image of our beautiful Savior, Jesus Christ.

## TODAY'S ACTION STEP

Examine your heart right now. Are you guilty of "ant slinging"? Think about the conversations you have with others, the posts you share on social media, and the ways you use God's Word. The truth of God's Word should be first and foremost applied to our own hearts. Is this the case for you?

Do you see how the enemy can use our frustrations with others' behavior to distract us from dealing with our own issues? What steps of obedience to God's Word have you neglected? Take time to write these down and repent of ignoring His commands. This week, anytime you are tempted to be distracted by someone else's sin, realign your focus to the areas in your own heart on which God has placed His finger. Commit to an undistracted focus on your own heart over the remainder of this forty-day journey.

# DAY 9.
# Can I Tell You a Secret?

*The secret of the Lord is with them that fear him; and he will shew them his covenant.*
Psalm 25:14 (KJV)

"Can I tell you a secret?" Chances are, you've had someone ask you that very question before. And if you're like me, your response to such a provocative question is to lean in and get a little excited.

Maybe it's a pregnancy no one else knows about, or a surprise engagement you hear about first. Either way, it's fun to be privy to knowledge others don't yet have. I have to giggle every time I see someone announce big news on social media and then I read the comments from close friends that say, "FINALLY! It's been killing me to hold this in!" I think (if we are honest), we like others to know we knew it first.

It's nice to feel the intimacy connected to being told a secret. When someone shares information with you that few others know, it usually means they trust you. It means there's an affection for you that provokes them to invite you to view the behind-the-scenes parts of their lives. Undoubtedly, this makes you feel special.

So the big question is, "Does God keep secrets?" Do some people get intimate knowledge of the Lord's plans that others don't?

I can tell you with confidence that the answer to these questions is a big, fat "YES!" Scripture makes it very clear on numerous occasions that the Lord shares behind-the-scenes information with certain individuals, unlocking mysteries in His Word that others cannot understand.

Today's verse is found in Psalm 25:14. I want you to read it in several translations:

*The secret of the Lord is with them that fear him; and he will shew them his covenant.* (KJV)

*The Lord confides in those who fear him; he makes his covenant known to them.* (NIV)

*The secret counsel of the Lord is for those who fear Him, and He reveals His covenant to them.* (HCSB)

*The Lord is a friend to those who fear him. He teaches them his covenant.* (NLT)

*The intimate counsel of the Lord is for those who fear him so they may know his covenant.* (ISV)

We see real-life examples of God "sharing secrets" appearing often in Scripture. For example, the Lord asks Himself (yes, even God talks to Himself) this question in Genesis 18:17–19a (NLT): *"Should I hide my plan from Abraham?" the Lord asked. "For Abraham will certainly become a great and mighty nation, and all the nations of the earth will be blessed through him. I have singled him out so that he will direct his sons and their families to keep the way of the Lord by doing what is right and just."* God singled out Abraham. He favored him with special knowledge of the future.

We see this happen also in the New Testament. After pulling the disciples aside (as He frequently did), Jesus made this shocking statement in Matthew 13:11 (NLT): *He replied, 'You are permitted to understand the secrets' of the Kingdom of Heaven, but others are not.'"* It may surprise you to begin to note how often Jesus intentionally kept certain information to Himself when around a crowd, while later explaining intimate details about the future or God's Word to His disciples when no one else was around.

Wouldn't it be nice to know the heart and mind of God? Wouldn't it be comforting to have God confide in you, giving you answers to your life's questions, often even before the test?

How does one receive this kind of counsel? The answer is found in the rest of Jesus' statement in Matthew 13:11–12 (NLT) *"You are permitted to understand the secrets of the Kingdom of Heaven, but others are not. To those who listen to my teaching, more understanding will be given, and they will have an abundance of knowledge. But for those who are not listening, even what little understanding they have will be taken away from them."*

This intimate knowledge is reserved for those who listen—not to those who merely hear, but to those who truly listen and obey. To those who "fear the Lord." Close secrets between friends imply covenant. It's a mutual understanding of deep relationship.

Have you ever shared an important detail of your life with someone who was indifferent to it? Have you ever poured your heart out to someone, only to realize that they didn't really share your excitement or concern? It's hurtful. I bet you didn't rush back to that person the next time you wanted a confidant!

Our relationship with God is no different. God desires friendship with us. Not one-sided, selfish friendship, wherein we present our wish list and honey-do's for Him to fulfill. He desires true, covenant relationship. He shares His heart and we listen. We obey. We fear.

Today, if you feel the silence of God, if you feel a wall between you and the Father, perhaps you should ask yourself what you might have done with what He's already given you. Ask yourself if you have listened and obeyed what you already know to do.

In my own life, I have noticed a pattern of silence and an inability to discern God's voice when I have neglected to follow through with certain instructions I have already been given. When I feel this "wall" or "veil" (see 2 Corinthians 3:13–18) between the Word and myself, I have learned to immediately begin examining myself for an area of disobedience or incomplete obedience. What have I done with what God has already spoken?

Today, if you hear God's voice, don't harden your heart (Hebrews 3:15). Have "ears to hear" (Mark 4) and listen! The God who spoke the universe into existence desires to equip you, instruct you, and open your mind to understand the "mysteries of the kingdom" (Luke 8:10), but this knowledge is birthed out of intimacy and obedience. Why struggle through life when the Holy Spirit yearns to walk through it WITH YOU, making known His plans, instructing and guiding you through His Word?

Friend, there is no greater honor than to know and really understand God's heart. *"The law you have revealed is more important to me than thousands of pieces of gold and silver"* (Psalm 119:72, NET). There is nothing more valuable than this intimacy. Nothing that brings us more peace. It's not aloof or far-off, not reserved for a spiritual elite group of people, but it is simply for those "with ears to hear."

## TODAY'S ACTION STEP

Take time to reflect on your relationship with Jesus. Think about your prayer life and be honest with yourself. Are your prayers selfish? Is your relationship with God one-sided and self-absorbed? Do you listen to HIS heart through His commands, or do you merely share yours? Is your relationship with the Father shallow or intimate? Does it provoke Him to share or hide the secrets of His heart?

Do you have unfinished business with God, or are there areas in which you haven't fully obeyed His voice? Take a minute to ask the Lord if there are any things that are hindering your relationship with Him, and then commit to making those things right so that you can be fully restored to true intimacy and friendship with the Father.

# DAY 10.
## Don't Fuss Between Bites

*But they soon forgot His works and they waited not for His counsel.*
Psalm 106:13 (NLT)

Often, being a mom teaches me about being a child of God. Since I am a mother of four, I am afforded plenty of opportunities to learn!

My husband and I have three beautiful girls and one boy. (We call him our "only begotten son.") It's humorous how different he is from our girls, and it's been this way since his birth.

Our daughters were born just barely hitting the six-pound mark; whereas, our son was nearly nine pounds! All three of the girls struggled to gain weight as infants, with their dainty, girlish appetites. Our giant son came out of the womb ready to eat and never looked back. As a matter of fact, when it came time to introduce him to solid foods, he was eating like a pro just a few days after opening wide to his first bite. I recall watching him get so excited about mushed peas that between each bite he would kick his many-rolled legs, flail his fat little arms, and fuss at me to hurry up. I had to laugh! I couldn't get the food in his mouth fast enough and he was letting me know!

On one such occasion, dinnertime quickly turned from humorous to frustrating, as my little fat man refused to be consoled about my inability to keep up with his hunger demands.

And then—as God so lovingly tends to do—He interrupted this normal mommy moment to teach me about myself. Just as I was consoling my frustrated man-child, trying to reason with a four-month-old about how irrational he was acting, I heard the Spirit of God whisper to my heart: "Melodi, don't fuss between bites."

I knew what the Lord was trying to say!

The step of faith we took to leave all that was familiar and plant a church halfway across the United States had not been all peaches and cream. While it has been super-exciting, grace-covered, miraculous-filled, and God-ordained, it has at times also been nerve-racking, fear-inducing, and self-doubt-raising. Let's just be real. For every mountaintop spiritual moment, there have been many real-life aggravations, lack, delay, interruptions, and disappointments. That's life.

At the same time as my four-month-old was very impatiently worrying over his next bite of food, I was struggling with worry over concerns about our upcoming church plant. *Where will we find the money to start a church? How will we start a church when we don't know anyone in this community? Where will the laborers come from? How will we afford the equipment? What if our family cannot financially survive such a big step of faith?* These were very real concerns. I had to DAILY surrender my tendency to worry.

I remember the Lord bringing me to Psalm 106:12–13 (NIV, emphasis added): "*Then they (the children of Israel) believed His Words; they sang His praise. But they SOON FORGOT His works and they WAITED NOT for His counsel.*" In a sense, the children of Israel "fussed between bites."

How sad that three days after the children of Israel were miraculously delivered from the slavery of Egypt, even through the middle of the Red Sea, they forgot. Three days after dancing and singing and rejoicing in God, they forgot. THREE DAYS! God didn't even have time to put the spoon back in the bowl and put it to their mouths again before they began to run those same mouths against Him.

They "soon forgot." The word "soon" in Strong's Concordance is translated most literally "to be liquid or to flow easily." In other words, their faith had holes in it. It paints a picture of a leaky cup. God deposited faith in them (backed up by miraculous power), but they allowed the circumstances they were in to let it leak out.

They "waited not." That word "waited" means in the Hebrew "to adhere or to cling." They failed to cling to what God had promised for them. He promised not only to deliver them out of their slavery, but to bring them to the Promised Land. Where was their memory of what He had already done?

How challenging!

How many times have we just shortly come off of a miracle of provision, joy, relationship breakthrough, deliverance, or personal freedom, only to "three days later" find ourselves complaining that we don't know what God is doing anymore! Lord, help us!

If we are honest, there usually isn't that much space between our last miracle and our current freak-out.

Through the years since God spoke to me that night, we have seen many miracles of provision. He DID, in fact, provide for every concern and question I had about that step of faith. We have witnessed one supernatural miracle after another. But what I have come to realize is that every new season presents itself with a new problem. Despite how often I see His faithfulness to act, I still have to choose to trust Him with every new "impossible" circumstance that provokes me to worry.

The reality is, there may be moments when I may not see Him spoon-in-hand. I may not see the food approaching my mouth. I may not know where the next provision will come from. But it is in those waiting and trusting seasons that I cannot forget about what He's already done. If He was faithful with the last bite—He will be faithful with the next.

I must let the memories of yesterday's miracles neutralize today's worries. At the times when I am most afraid, I must cling to the faithfulness of God to complete His promises. Because He knows my needs, controls everything, and loves me so deeply, I can rest contentedly between bites. That is the beautiful privilege of being called a child of God.

## TODAY'S ACTION STEP

Have you been guilty of "fussing between bites?" Do today's problems cause you to quickly forget yesterday's miracles? Read Jesus' words in Matthew 6:25–33. Take some time to recall ways in which God has provided for you in the past. Write down some of those miracles. In prayer, bring your needs to the Father and then confidently leave them in His capable hands.

# DAY 11.
# Eye Exam

*Make sure that the light you think you have is not actually darkness.*
Luke 11:35 (NLT)

I recently read a news article about a woman who was scheduled to have routine cataract surgery on her eyes. The woman complained of dry eye and discomfort that she attributed to "old age." However, as the doctors began her surgery, they noticed mucus-covered blue objects in her eyes. Upon further examination, they realized one of the objects in her eye was actually seventeen old contact lenses that had fused together! They went on to find an additional ten contacts fused together elsewhere in her eye.

Pardon me for saying this, but...HUH????!!

I wear contacts. I have since I was in the eighth grade, and I'm not really sure how you could forget to remove twenty-seven contact lenses from your eye. Bless her heart. The woman's eyes hadn't suffered additional damage from the contact lenses, but obviously, her cataract surgery had to be rescheduled.

This news article reminded me of a sobering statement Jesus made in Luke 11, beginning in verse 34 (NLT): "*Your eye is like a lamp that provides light for your body. When your eye is healthy, your whole body is filled with light. But when it is unhealthy, your body is filled with darkness. Make sure that the light you think you have is not actually darkness. If you are filled with light, with no dark corners, then your whole life will be radiant, as though a floodlight were filling you with light."*

Every time I read these verses, I am reminded of the times in my life when I walked around squinting, spiritually blinded to my own faults and depravity. Despite being trapped in repeated, life-dominating sins that lurked in the dark corners of my heart, I still managed to simultaneously attend church, quote scripture passages, and even lead various ministries. It is unfortunately easy to walk in self-deception. It's easy to compartmentalize our lives and ignore layers upon layers of sin that build up over time.

I find the biblical symbolism and connection between the eyes and our freedom fascinating. At the apostle Paul's conversion to Christianity, we are told that "immediately, something like scales" fell off his eyes (Acts 9:18). Jesus said that it is possible for us to walk around disabled by a plank in our eye, all-the-while hyper-fixating on the speck in our brother's. He warned that the hardness of our hearts can cause spiritual blindness, making us incapable of seeing truth, even if it's presented plainly before us. He described people who, although *"they look, but they don't really see. They hear, but they don't really listen or understand"* (Matthew 13:13, NLT).

*Make sure that the light you think you have is not actually darkness.* What a sobering statement!

So, how do we avoid this? Even more pertinent, how do we know whether we are currently walking in spiritual deception? I think the key to checking our sight is found in verse 36 (NLT): *"If you are filled with light, with no dark corners, then your whole life will be radiant."*

Filled with light. No dark corners. Hiding nothing. Free of duplicity and pretense. Hearts open before our Father.

Many times, we lack the courage to be honest with ourselves. We rationalize or ignore the plank in our eye, distracting ourselves with others' mistakes. This 40-day ARISE Journey is about SELF-EXPOSING DARK CORNERS. God is such a beautifully merciful God. He never desires to expose our weaknesses or humiliate us. I heard someone once say that God will always deal with us in private before exposing us in public. He desires that we ourselves fling open every dark corner of our hearts and expose them to the light of His Word.

By nature, we all hide sin. We have been doing it since the original sin in the Garden of Eden. John 3:19b–21 (NLT) says, *"God's light came into the world, but people loved the darkness more than the light, for their actions were evil. All who do evil hate the light and refuse to go near it for fear their sins will be exposed. But those who do what is right come to the light so others can see that they are doing what God wants."*

Those who do what's right come to the light. They welcome the light of the Word, even if it leaves them somewhat naked and vulnerable before a holy God. Regardless of how uncomfortable the confession of our failures can be, there is no other way to true freedom. Our spiritual walk will always be stalled at the point of our duplicity. We can go no further until we lay bare our weaknesses and allow God to peel back every layer of deception and sin.

Do you truly want to be set free? Bring everything into the light. Expose every dark corner. Refuse to be blackmailed by the condemnation in which your sin has trapped you. Allow God to shine on your heart and bring His radiance. He is waiting to give you sight again.

## TODAY'S ACTION STEP

Take time to ask yourself some hard questions and be open to an eye exam from the Lord:

Are you the same person in private as you are in public? Do you have any dark corners in your heart? Are there layers of lies you have told yourself to justify your sin?

Begin to confess your faults to the Father, acknowledging any areas of hypocrisy. Ask Him to cleanse and free you completely. Commit now to being completely honest with yourself during this journey so that your spiritual growth is not stunted.

# DAY 12.
# Sticky Trap

*See to it that no one comes short of the grace of God; that no root of bitterness springing up causes trouble, and by it many be defiled.*
Hebrews 12:15 (NASB)

Have you ever seen a mouse caught in a sticky trap? It's pretty pitiful.

I don't like rodents. I wouldn't dare hold a mouse or play with it. I don't want them in my house, and I don't think they are cute. BUT (*call me a softy*), I feel bad when I see any animal caught in a trap—even the gross ones.

I remember when we first moved into a new home in Louisiana. The house had been unoccupied for nine months, and the previous owners had left food scraps in the pantry. We cleaned the home really well and moved our things in, but on the very first night, we heard scurrying noises. You guessed it. Mice. (*Pardon me as I gag.*) To make matters worse, our bed had not yet been put together, so we were sleeping on mattresses on the floor.

All night long, I had nightmares of mice chewing off my baby's toes and crawling into my hair!

I sent the hubby to the store in the middle of the night for traps. He set out the sticky traps with a little peanut butter, and the next morning we saw that we had caught three mice. I was both horrified and relieved. There was just one problem: They were still alive—squeaking and pulling to no avail, awaiting their doom.

They had been caught in a very sticky trap, and it was their downfall. Honestly (*don't judge me!*), I cried. I felt so bad for the little disgusting things!

It's tough to watch something get snared. It's even tougher when it's people whom you know and love. Today, I want to talk about what I feel is the stickiest trap of all, what I consider to be one of the most effective weapons in the enemy's arsenal: bitterness and offense.

The writer of Hebrews warns of its dangers in chapter twelve (NASB) when it says, "*See to it that no one comes short of the grace of God; that no root of bitterness springing up causes trouble, and by it many be defiled.*"

There are two words in this verse that strike fear in my heart: "many" and "defiled." I have seen this deadly scheme of the enemy over and over in the years I have served in ministry. I have watched this sticky trap take down even those I considered to be spiritual giants. What might have started as a hurt or a misunderstanding, grew and festered, until it consumed and defiled, rendering its victim unusable by the Lord.

The word "offense" is translated in Strong's Concordance like this: "*Offense—skándalon—the trigger of a trap (the mechanism, closing a trap down on the unsuspecting victim); (figuratively) an offense, putting a negative cause-and-effect relationship into motion.*"

An offense can come in both the personal form (something wrong done to you) or the borrowed variety (something wrong done to someone you love). Please understand that a borrowed or inherited offense is often worse than a personal one and is frequently compounded by misinformation. Either way, it's a trap. And it's a sticky one!

Want to know whether you are in harm's way? I've listed some symptoms of an offended spirit:

1.  **Jealousy and Insecurity**—Reading into things (i.e., feeling rejected when you are not invited to an event or when you are not recognized for what you do).
2.  **Control/Manipulation and Selfishness**—Having to have your way or taking things personally.
3.  **Negativity/Having a Critical Spirit**—Believing the worst about others.
4.  **Outbursts of Anger**
5.  **Touchiness**—Leaving people feeling like they must walk on eggshells around you.
6.  **Gossip/Slander**—Frequently talking about old wounds to others (often bringing up offenses from months or even years back), needing to validate yourself to have others on your side). Often masks as sarcasm or passive-aggressiveness.
7.  **A Martyr Complex**—Claiming to have forgiven but bringing offenses up often in order to receive sympathy from others.
8.  **An Attitude of Entitlement**—Feeling that you are owed something, instead of laying down your rights, as Christ did.

Strong's Concordance translates the word "defiled" in the above verse this way: "*to dye with another color, to stain, to defile, pollute, sully, contaminate, soil.*" The word "trouble" is described in Strong's Concordance like this: "*to crowd in, i.e., (figuratively) to annoy: of the growth of a poisonous plant.*"

The bottom line is that a damaged, defiled root produces poisonous, toxic fruit. Offense is a sticky trap in which you don't want to get caught! It will lure you in with promises of justification and fairness, convincing you that releasing your offender is the same as endorsing or enabling him or her. All the while, you are actually the one being defiled, strangled by the bitter root growing around the walls of your heart.

*Sister, you cannot be free and forgiven until you free and forgive others.*

For this journey to be a success, you must completely release any area of bitterness in your heart. As a matter of fact, Jesus took reconciliation with our brothers and sisters so seriously that He said this:

> *But if you do not forgive others their sins, your Father will not forgive your sins.* (Matthew 6:15, NIV)

> *So if you are offering your gift at the altar and there remember that your brother has something against you, leave your gift there before the altar and go. First be reconciled to your brother, and then come and offer your gift.* (Matthew 5:23–24, ESV)

So, how do we forgive and release? First, recognize that no offense is worth defiling your heart. Second, remember how much Christ has forgiven you. When you are tempted to hold on to wrongs that others have inflicted, begin to thank Jesus for the price He paid for you. Third, pray for the person with whom you are offended. It is difficult not to begin to love someone you pray for regularly. As you commit them to prayer, God will change your heart to see that person as He does. Lastly, remember that forgiveness is a process and not an event. You will need to daily rebuke and take captive any thought of bitterness or resentment. When practical, even consider "punishing the thought" of unforgiveness by choosing to bless your offender in some way.

I've been in women's ministry long enough to understand the kind of offenses that are sitting on the other side of this book: trauma and abuse that have been devastating and may seem impossible to release. But I also know that if the cross of Jesus was enough to pay for my sin and for yours, it can cover theirs, too. I am praying for you to find peace and freedom in total forgiveness. *You can do this*, through Christ who gives you strength.

## TODAY'S ACTION STEP

Be honest before the Lord. Are you caught in the sticky trap of offense? Today, read Matthew 18:15–35 and journal what God is speaking to you. Take time to pray for anyone toward whom you may feel hurt or bitterness. Ask God to bless them and give you the strength to completely release them through the power of the cross. Remember that forgiveness is not a one-time event, and you will need to repeat the steps outlined in today's devotion every time you are tempted with thoughts of unforgiveness.

*ARISE! by Melodi Hawley*

# DAY 13.
# Playing Church

*Examine yourselves to see whether you are in the faith; test yourselves. Do you not realize that Christ Jesus is in you—unless, of course, you fail the test?*
2 Corinthians 13:5 (NIV)

My husband Brandon was a true "church kid;" he teases that he "cut his teeth on a church pew." His grandmother told me one particularly adorable story about a time when he was around four years old. He lined up his stuffed animals on his bed and was caught "preaching" to them. He even had an altar call, laid hands on the sick and they recovered, and two teddy bears asked Jesus to be their Savior. It was a stuffed animal revival!

I love that story. I think many church kids grow up playing church, and it's beautiful.

Unless the pretending never stops.

Unfortunately (and especially in the Bible belt of this country), many "Christians" learn how to "play church" instead of pursuing an authentic relationship with Christ.

They are master mimickers: reciting Scripture, wearing Christian T-shirts, posting religious memes full of "hallelujahs" and "amens." But upon close examination of the life behind the curtain, there is no true fruit. To their families and to those who know them best, they are pretenders. Imposters. Posers.

Sadly, they are often the last to realize this. The shroud of pretense has convinced them that their words alone are enough.

They have pretended so well that they have become drunk on their own delusion.

Scripture describes them like this: "*You should know this, Timothy, that in the last days there will be very difficult times. For people will love only themselves and their money. They will be boastful and proud, scoffing at God, disobedient to their parents, and ungrateful. They will consider nothing sacred. They will be unloving and unforgiving; they will slander others and have no self-control. They will be cruel and hate what is good. They will betray their friends, be reckless, be puffed up with pride, and love pleasure rather than God. They will act religious, but they will reject the power that could make them godly. Stay away from people like that!*" (2 Timothy 3:1–5, NLT).

I have such a burden for the American Church. We have bred a generation of pretenders, accumulated a mass of followers who bear the name of Christ, but deny Him the authority to run their lives, thereby rendering them impotent. Powerless. Void of the life of God.

We have reduced the "sinner's prayer" to a magical phrase to repeat as fire insurance. There's not much talk of denying yourself or taking up your cross and following Jesus. Rather, we have grown accustomed to a weak faith, shallow Christianity, and a hollow religion. It is now the norm.

I know this sounds harsh, and I pray you hear my heart. My desire is not to criticize, but rather to encourage you to examine your life. These words of Jesus bring a deep sense of urgency to my heart: "*Not everyone who says to me, 'Lord, Lord,' will enter the kingdom of heaven, but only the one who does the will of my Father who is in heaven. Many will say to me on that day, 'Lord, Lord, did we not prophesy in your name and in your name drive out demons and in your name perform many miracles?' Then I will tell them plainly, 'I never knew you. Away from me, you evildoers!'*" (Matthew 7:21–23, NIV).

"*Many.*"

This breaks me. The reality is that playing church can't transform a life. <u>Christianity apart from a radical life commitment is merely a generic version, an imitation, a cheap knockoff brand</u>. It can do more harm than good because it lures people into having a false sense of security that being in the right place (i.e., church) and saying the right things (like, "I believe in Jesus") are equivalent to being right with God, and that's just simply not true.

In Ezekiel 33:31–33 (NLT), God says to His prophet, "*So my people come pretending to be sincere and sit before you. They listen to your words, but they have no intention of doing what you say. Their mouths are full of lustful words, and their hearts seek only after money. You are very entertaining to them, like someone who sings love songs with a beautiful voice or plays fine music on an instrument. They hear what you say, but they don't act on it! But when all these terrible things happen to them—as they certainly will—then they will know a prophet has been among them.*"

In Psalm 50:16b–17 (NLT), God says, "*Why bother reciting my decrees and pretending to obey my covenant? For you refuse my discipline and treat my words like trash.*"

The book of James cautions us that faith apart from works is dead. Real faith bears fruit. It's alive and kicking. Powerful. Life-changing. Radical. Discontent to remain stagnant and cold or lukewarm and complacent. Real faith in Jesus Christ consumes you from the inside out. Real faith WORKS!

Is your faith REAL? There's never been a more important question. Please don't assume that a prayer recited as a child without any accompanying life changes equates salvation! Jesus said that you would know real faith by the fruit it bears (Matthew 7:17-20).

So, I cannot neglect to ask this question: Are you TRULY saved? Do you truly know Jesus Christ? Have you surrendered the complete lordship of your life to Him? Is there evidence of real salvation?

Friends, the pretense isn't funny when it determines your eternal destiny. The scripture 2 Corinthians 13:5a (NIV) warns us, *"Examine yourselves to see whether you are in the faith; test yourselves."* I pray that you will take the time to really examine your life, and should you fail to find your faith genuine, make the decision TODAY to truly make Christ your Lord.

## TODAY'S ACTION STEP

Today may be the most important day of our journey together. None of us can afford to spend our lives merely "playing church". It is absolutely critical that you not pass this by haphazardly. Have you ever shown any evidence of true salvation, such as: 1) a sudden, radical life change; 2) a desire to please God and a new distaste for sin (not perfection, but your desires becoming different); or 3) an ability to understand God's Word? Scripture teaches that the lost are incapable of perceiving the Word of God because they are spiritually dead (see 1 Corinthians 2:14).

Perhaps after considering these questions, you feel you have never truly committed your life to Christ, but you desire to do so. If the Spirit of God is drawing your heart right now, He is as close as the mention of His name! His brutal death on the cross ensured that the penalty for your sins has already been paid. He offers you salvation as a free gift. He desires to enter into covenant relationship with you. I invite you to pray this prayer with me if you are serious about giving Him full control of your life:

*"God, I know that I'm a sinner. I have lived my life to please myself and have not followed Your commands. I understand that my sin has separated me from You. But I also believe that Jesus died on the cross to take my punishment. He paid what I owed. I*

*accept His gift of salvation, and I ask you to forgive me for my sins. I desire to enter into a covenant relationship with You, through the blood of Jesus Christ. I give You my heart and I make You the Lord of my life. I ask You to help me build my life upon the Rock of Your Word, and I thank You for saving me! In the name of Jesus I pray. Amen."*

# DAY 14.
# Grab the Cord!

*"For I know the plans I have for you," says the Lord. "They are plans for good and not for disaster, to give you a future and a hope. In those days when you pray, I will listen. If you look for Me wholeheartedly, you will find me. I will be found by you,"*
*says the Lord.*
Jeremiah 29:11–14 (NLT)

One of my favorite things to do in the summertime is to go whitewater rafting. We are privileged to live very near rafting country, where people from all over the world come to seek the adrenaline rush of the rapids. Not only is it one of my favorite activities in the world, but I especially get a kick out of taking newbies on the river. I love introducing fearful new friends to the excitement of the whitewater and watching their reactions as the raft pounds into its first class-five rapid!

I remember the first time I went rafting in West Virginia. The guide very pointedly warned, "Alright, people, this isn't Disney World. You CAN die!" In my somewhat morbid curiosity, I asked how often that happened. He explained that most often, the only people who die on the river are people who have preexisting medical conditions (like heart problems), or people who aren't "active participants in their own rescue."

When you go rafting, listening to the guides is crucial. They will tell you how hard and in which direction to paddle. They warn you prior to each new rapid and inform you of which way to swim, should you fall out of the boat. Because there are large rocks you need to avoid, you should never, ever put your feet down. If you do, your feet might get lodged in a crevice of a rock and the current could hold you under, potentially causing you to drown. Very importantly, should you fall out of the boat, you cannot just hang out and wait there for someone to come get you. You will be required to listen to instructions as you swim and grab hold of the guide's paddle when he or she tries to pull you back in. Simply put—you must be "an active participant in your own rescue."

In the very famous verses provided at the beginning of this devotional, we are told that God has a future and a HOPE for us. This word "hope" in the Hebrew is the word "tiqvah" and it is translated in its most literal form in Strong's Concordance as "a cord." What a word picture God is giving us by using this word! It's as if He is saying, "*I know the plans I have for you, plans to prosper you and not to harm you, to give you a future and a CORD to grab a hold of when you feel like your drowning!*"

I think that many people fail to realize that they have an active role in their own redemption. I think often we expect hope to grab us, pull us up, and do all the work. But, in reality, it's a CHOICE. We must be active participants in our own rescue. God is throwing us a lifeline; it's an effectual, highly efficient, gracious rescue plan, but it won't work without some sort of effort on our part.

So, why wouldn't we grab the cord of hope? Why would we choose to stay in our desperation and sin when the lifeline has been thrown?

For some, I believe it's because they can't see the cord. The waves have pounded them so fiercely, they can scarcely take a breath. Perhaps they've never had someone make them aware of such a hope. Romans 10:14 and 17 (NLT) says, "*But how can they call on Him to save them unless they believe in Him? And how can they believe in Him if they have never heard about Him? And how can they hear about Him unless someone tells them? //*

*So then faith comes by hearing, and hearing by the word of God."* This is why it's critical that we share the hope of God with those who are drowning in despair!

But I believe there is another deeper, darker reason that some don't grab hold of the hope of God. I think there are those who actually *prefer* to stay in the water. They have come to find identity in their distress. Growing fond of the sympathy their drama creates, they proudly wear their depravity like a badge.

*The water's warmer than the boat. It's familiar. I see the cord, but I don't know whether I even want out.*

In Acts 16:16–19 (NLT), we read a fascinating story told by Luke. Let's take a look at it.

> *One day as we were going down to the place of prayer, we met a demon-possessed slave girl. She was a fortune-teller who earned a lot of money for her masters. She followed Paul and the rest of us, shouting, "These men are servants of the Most High God, and they have come to tell you how to be saved." This went on day after day until Paul got so exasperated that he turned and said to the demon within her, "I command you in the Name of Jesus Christ to come out of her." And instantly it left her. Her masters' hopes of wealth were now shattered, so they grabbed Paul and Silas and dragged them before the authorities at the marketplace. "The whole city is in an uproar because of these Jews!" they shouted to the city officials.*

Immediately after this, Paul and Silas were thrown into prison. The people in that city were so angry that this slave girl had been freed that they locked up the apostles.

I really believe that some women in today's Church are like that slave girl. Notice that she said all the right things. She confessed the truth about God's messengers and His message. She even followed God's anointed around the village. But she was BOUND.

She was a slave to demonic bondage that profited from her remaining in shackles.

Some of you may say the right things. You know God's Word. You go to church. You hang out with other Christians. But in your heart of hearts, you know you are a slave to sin and bondage. The enemy is trying his hardest to convince you to STAY A SLAVE, to remain in the warm water, and to deny the chance of rescue because he will not profit from your freedom. Don't listen to him! He is a liar! There is nothing in that water but death!

On this journey, God's going to speak some HOLY HOPE into your life, but you must GRAB THE CORD and hold on! Determine that you are tired of drowning.

The rest of today's verse gives us a sacred promise: *"If you look for me wholeheartedly, you will find me. I will be found by you"* (Jeremiah 29:13–14, NLT). God promises to meet you at your point of effort. He pledges not only to throw the lifeline of hope to you, but also to do His part to pull you back in. Your rescue is on the other side of that cord. Commit today to grab it and hold on!

## TODAY'S ACTION STEP

This entire journey is really about being an "active participant in your own rescue." Are you willing to grab hold of the cord of hope? Search your heart right now. Can you be brutally honest with yourself? Are there areas of your depravity you still enjoy? Do you see that while your bondage may be comfortable, it is actually quite deadly? Take time to pray and ask God to help you see things as He sees them. Commit to doing your part throughout this journey to seeing yourself completely free.

# THE ARISE PHASE

*Awake, sleeper, and **arise from the dead**, And Christ will shine on you.*
Ephesians 5:14 (NASB)

Congratulations! You have made it to the second part of our journey: the Arise Phase. The next several devotionals will include practical steps to begin leaving behind destructive lifestyle patterns. If you have ever been guilty of hitting the snooze button and yelling, "I'm awake, I'm awake!" in an effort to stay in bed longer, you know that being awake simply isn't enough. We must rise up and begin to take action. Using God's Word as a guide, we will "get up and walk out" what we have learned from the Awaken Phase through practical, yet challenging biblical mandates.

Take time to watch a special message from the author before beginning the Arise Phase by visiting arisejourney.com/phasetwo.

# DAY 15.
# The Sound an Apple Tree Makes

*Planted in the house of the Lord, they will flourish in the courts
of our God. They will still bear fruit in old age.*
Psalm 92:13–14a (NIV)

Have you ever heard the sound an apple tree makes when it produces an apple?

After moving to West Virginia, I was surprised to find an abundance of naturally occurring apple trees. They are everywhere. On the corner of my street alone, there are several. I have an apple tree that grows in my backyard and every summer the side of our yard is filled with apples.

When I first moved here, it fascinated me—as did the summer fireflies, the constant mountain breeze, and the abundance of deer, bear, and other wildlife.

Even after five and a half years of living here, I still think it's amazing.

Which brings me back to my question: *"Have you ever heard the sound an apple tree makes when it produces an apple?"* After living with an apple tree in my yard for quite some time, I have discovered that if you lean in, get really close to the tree, put your ear next to the bark, close your eyes, and concentrate…

You hear nothing.

No straining, grunting, groaning, or snorting. Apple trees don't make noise as they make apples. This is because apple making is effortless to a healthy apple tree. It doesn't need to strive or work to produce its fruit; the fruit is a natural by-product of a healthy tree.

We all want to produce good fruit. Jesus said we would be able to tell the condition of a person's heart by the fruit produced in his or her life. However, we each have undoubtedly had moments when we've produced something less than satisfactory: Rotten, selfish, icky behaviors that embarrassingly come out at times.

Sometimes we produce unpleasant fruit even when are trying not to! If you're like me, you have felt the frustration of genuinely trying to do your best and falling short. If you were to listen to the sound of your soul at those times, you would likely hear anything but silence. You'd hear striving. Straining. Struggling. Flailing. You'd say that the production of "good fruit" was *anything* but effortless.

But it shouldn't be this way. The production of good fruit should be spontaneous. Beautiful. Natural.

So how do we organically produce good fruit without striving? It's a process that doesn't happen by changing the behavior itself. Fixing wrong "fruit" has nothing to do with behavior modification or self-help. Jesus said this: "*A good tree produces good fruit, and a bad tree produces bad fruit. A good tree can't produce bad fruit, and a bad tree can't produce good fruit*" (Matthew 7:17–18, NLT).

All the good intentions in the world won't change moral decay or fix the bad spots in our hearts. The only thing that can rectify a withering branch is reconnecting it to a healthy source. If the branch is connected to a healthy source, it will consistently and beautifully produce good fruit.

Scripture tells us that this type of good growth happens in two ways:

**1. By abiding in Christ and His Word.** Consistent, daily time spent in God's Word is a nonnegotiable requirement. Jesus is the Word "made flesh." If you want to meet Jesus face-to-face, then simply pick up the Word of God. Christ said, *"Remain in me, and I will remain in you. For a branch cannot produce fruit if it is severed from the vine, and you cannot be fruitful unless you remain in Me. Yes, I am the vine; you are the branches. Those who remain in Me, and I in them, will produce much fruit. For apart from Me you can do nothing"* (John 15:4–5, NLT).

If an area of your life is unfruitful or is even producing negative fruit, chances are it is not connected to the Word of God via your consistent obedience. Find out what God's Word says and do it—not merely for a day or for a month, but apply it consistently, every day. Give God's Word time to seep deep into that area and bear beautiful fruit in the proper season. You will be surprised to find life budding forth without your effort: financial concerns rectified, relationships healed, strongholds broken, peace and joy commonplace—all occurring without your striving.

**2. Plant yourself in the house of God.** Psalm 92:13–14 (NIV) says, *"Planted in the house of the Lord, they will flourish in the courts of our God. They will still bear fruit in old age."* I cannot overstate the importance of digging in and planting yourself in a life-giving church. The Word says that God's Church is "His body" and that He is the head. Many people try to "go rogue" and live their lives isolated, feeling they can make it on their own. This is simply not true. You cannot separate Christ from His Church.

Pretend for a minute that my husband loved me—but he only paid attention to my head. He completely ignored the rest of my body. There would be no procreation. No fruit. Nada. Likewise, you will NEVER bear fruit that remains without planting yourself in the house of God. And the more you serve, dig in, and involve yourself in that local church, the more fruit you will bear. The deeper the roots, the sweeter the fruit!

God designed us to need one another. Satan wants to isolate you—to get you focused on your local church's flaws or problems—because you are an easy target when you are standing alone. Don't fall for his trap! Find a local church that holds the Word of God as the supreme standard, get involved in that church body, and JUST WATCH the beautiful, effortless fruit that will result.

Fruit bearing is organic when we commit to abiding in the Word and planting in God's house. If you are straining and striving today in an area of your life, step back and evaluate whether or not that area is truly connected to the Vine.

## TODAY'S ACTION STEP

Let's do a fruit inspection: What type of fruit are you producing? If the answer is less than satisfactory, evaluate yourself. Are you planted daily in God's Word? Are you planted in God's house, or are you independent-spirited?

This week, your challenge is to spend time in God's Word every day. I also challenge you to go to church every chance you get this month. (This includes to midweek services or any small groups that you can attend.) Step out in faith and get involved in an area at your church by serving behind the scenes in some capacity. You will be surprised at how much you enjoy planting and flourishing!

# DAY 16.
# What's Your Kryptonite?

*Above all else, guard your heart, for everything you do flows from it.*
Proverbs 4:23 (NIV)

I'm not a comic book junkie. Really, I couldn't tell you much about any of the comic book superheroes. I remember watching The Avengers and being completely lost, thinking, *I guess you have to know the backstory of these characters to get this!*

But even *I* know about kryptonite. I remember the old 1980s Superman movies, in which I first learned about this fictional material that was the great superhero's only weakness. The word "kryptonite" has become a catchphrase for a type of Achilles' heel, the one weakness of an otherwise invulnerable hero.

I don't know about you, but I'm no superhero. And to be honest, I have far more than just one weakness; my list of weaknesses would probably be (at least) two pages long! But as I came across a familiar story in Scripture, I pondered the idea that many of us really DO have a spiritual kryptonite (if you will)—one area that tends to trip us up or cause us to fall.

Mark 10:17–22 (NLT) recounts the following story:

> *As Jesus was starting out on his way to Jerusalem, a man came running up to him, knelt down, and asked, "Good Teacher, what must I do to inherit eternal life?" "Why do you call me good?" Jesus asked. "Only God is truly good. But to answer your*

*question, you know the commandments: 'You must not murder. You must not commit adultery. You must not steal. You must not testify falsely. You must not cheat anyone. Honor your father and mother.'" "Teacher," the man replied, "I've obeyed all these commandments since I was young." Looking at the man, Jesus felt genuine love for him. "There is still one thing you haven't done," he told him. "Go and sell all your possessions and give the money to the poor, and you will have treasure in heaven. Then come, follow me." At this the man's face fell, and he went away sad, for he had many possessions.*

This story is so tragic to me. This young ruler was filled with enthusiasm and zeal. I believe he really DID love the Lord and that he desired to go after God. And yet…his money was his kryptonite. It was the one thing he loved more than God, and thus, it was the very thing that became his downfall.

Part of the reason this story breaks my heart is that I see it frequently repeated in the lives of those around me. In ministry, we get attached to many precious people who are full of zeal and passion. They begin their spiritual walks with enthusiasm and a genuine desire to please God. And then…Satan finds that ONE THING they love more than God.

If I were to ask them, *"Do you love* (enter their personal type of kryptonite here) *more than God?"* they would likely be quick to deny it. Yet their lives testify to the fact that this one thing is what's really sitting on the throne of their hearts. It is the line in the sand that their obedience to God cannot cross. *God, You can have all of me…but just not this,* they pray. They hide this area from their spiritual leaders and their families, rationalizing why what they are doing is not wrong and then become highly defensive (or even leave the church) if this area is brought into the light.

Spiritual kryptonite can come in many forms: seeking attention, bad relationships, money, drugs, success, fame, the inability to receive correction, pornography, alcohol, and (dare I say it?) even sleep. It can be anything—anything that you love more than God (as evidenced by an inability to surrender this area to God).

We have all seen great men and women fall. We have watched as sexual affairs have taken down even the greatest of spiritual giants. We have seen how the love of money or power corrupts leaders who were once defined by integrity. We have seen passionate servants of Christ overdose and die in moments of weakness and depravity. What happened? Slowly, subtly, Satan convinced them that they could compartmentalize their hearts.

Friend, do not let the enemy snare you in this web of deception! God wants ALL of you! He alone belongs on the throne of your heart! Proverbs 4:23 (NIV) says, *"Above all else, guard your heart, for everything you do flows from it."* That word "guard" means to "garrison" or "put up a defensive fortress" around it.

If God is putting His finger on an area of your life, do not be deceived into thinking that you can hold on to it and not have it ultimately infect the rest of your life! We must stop rationalizing, justifying, and making excuses for why we can hold on to this "one thing" and still be okay. We must live lives of *total surrender*—yielding every area of our affections in obedience to God's Word.

In the Garden of Eden, God told Cain (a man who was struggling with the kryptonite of jealousy and bitterness): *"Why do you look so dejected? You will be accepted if you do what is right. But if you refuse to do what is right, then watch out! Sin is crouching at the door, eager to control you. But you must subdue it and be its master"* (Genesis 4:6–7, NLT).

Only you can decide what will rule you. Today, I beg you not to "walk away sad" as did that rich young ruler who "almost" gave it all to God. Let me promise you this: Once you finally release that one thing, you will experience freedom like you have never known before, realizing that your kryptonite was never worth your heart in the first place! You will understand the absolute peace that comes from a life fully surrendered to God.

## TODAY'S ACTION STEP

Take some time to sit still before God and be honest with yourself. Is there an area on which God has placed His finger as you have read today's devotional? What is your kryptonite? If God reveals an area of weakness to you, take a bold step of faith and ask for help from a mature Christian friend. Be willing to be vulnerable and confess that weakness to a spiritual leader or a peer you can trust. Ask them to keep you accountable to surrendering this area to God.

# DAY 17.
# Monkey-See, Monkey-Do

*They followed the example of the nations around them,*
*disobeying the Lord's command not to imitate them.*
2 Kings 17:15c (NLT)

I have a nearly two-year-old daughter who is a little mockingbird. It is so humorous to watch her attempt to say "grown-up" words and do "grown-up" things, although, in many ways, it is sobering! If you want to see a mirror of your actions, invite a two-year-old to hang out with you for the day. You may be surprised to find out a few things you didn't know about yourself!

Much of what we learn in life is by imitation. Monkey-see, monkey-do is how we learn to function in our surroundings—by watching others and imitating what we see them doing. This is subconscious. Rarely are we even aware that we are playing a game of social Simon Says, digesting and imitating the actions of those around us.

We are copycats by design. In all reality, very little of what we do is truly individual. We are mostly a melting pot of our external influences. This is the reason it is vital that we choose carefully what environment in which we immerse ourselves.

The children of Israel made a detrimental mistake: They copied the customs of the world AROUND them rather than the decrees of the God INSIDE OF them, and it cost them greatly. Second Kings 17:15 (NLT) says this: *"They rejected his decrees and the covenant he had made with their ancestors and they despised all his warnings. They worshiped worthless idols so they became worthless themselves. They followed the example of the nations around them, disobeying the Lord's command not to imitate them."*

That is strong wording! The word "worthless" here means "polluted or defiled." They became this way by imitating the world around them.

God's Word says that we are to "*Come out from them and be separate*" (2 Corinthians 6:17, NIV). The very definition of the word "holy" is to be "set apart" for His service. Jesus called us the "light of the world." But how can God use us as a city on a hill, shining our light for a dark world to see, if we are ourselves immersed in darkness?

My question for you today is: "*Who are you imitating?*" When others look at you, do you stand apart? Or is your life marked by the same addiction, depression, drama, darkness, or confusion present in the world around you? When others see the way you respond to fear, trauma, or hurt, does it glorify Christ?

Undeniably, you are acting like whomever or whatever you have surrounded yourself with, whether you realize it or not. What you ingest, you become. (You are what you eat, if you will.) Make no mistake about it: The movies you watch, the music you listen to (take a second and REALLY listen to those lyrics!), the conversations you allow yourself to be a part of—all of it matters.

I am not advocating a spiritual elitism that makes us irrelevant to the world. Lost people should not hate us because we act too "spiritual" for them. However, do not make the mistake of thinking that you can walk like, talk like, dress like, or act like a lost world and still adequately maintain your influence in the Kingdom of God. People aren't buying what you're selling if what you're SAYING isn't backed up by how you're LIVING!

In the book of Acts, the early Church made a radical, costly choice: They evaluated themselves and "cleaned out their closets," so to speak, in order to eliminate anything that hindered their walk with Christ. Check out Acts 19:19 (NLT): *"A number of them who had been practicing sorcery brought their incantation books and burned them at a public bonfire. The value of the books was several million dollars."* Several million dollars! The reality is that choosing to follow Christ wholeheartedly will cost you! It will mean the severing of toxic relationships, sinful habits, and ungodly interests from your life. It will mean separating yourself from that which defiles or pollutes you.

If you are consistently failing to act like Christ, perhaps it is because you have surrounded yourself with things that are "anti-Christ" (or against the Word of Christ). Right now, I challenge you to be honest with yourself. Are there any things (or people) from which you need to separate yourself so that you will be truly "set apart"?

## TODAY'S ACTION STEP

Who are you (subconsciously) imitating? What is influencing your behavior? Today, walk around your home and look through your streaming media, your phone's search history, and your social media posts. Does what you find there glorify Christ? With whom are you spending the majority of your time? What comes out of their mouths? Is it life or death? Take time to ask God if there are any relationships from which you need to distance yourself, any environments from which you need to run, or any influences from which you need to be cut off. Be willing to make that hard choice today. Clean out your closets like the church in the book of Acts did, even if it costs you greatly. Choose to put God first above all else, so that He can truly use you as a light in the darkness.

# DAY 18.
# Can You Hear Me Now?

*Today, if you will hear His voice, harden not your hearts.*
Hebrews 4:7b (NASB)

I need to have my children's hearing checked again. My kids have exhibited some peculiar symptoms that are leading me to believe they may have what is known as Selective Hearing Syndrome. For instance, their ears are strangely hyperalert to words like "candy" and "presents," while their ability to hear phrases like "clean up" and "do your homework" have been devastatingly diminished. It's quite strange.

The other day, I was looking at the beautiful blond hair on the back of my oldest daughter's head and said, "Eden, please hand me that." She didn't budge. Surely, she could hear me; she was only two feet away!

But nothing.

When I rebuked her, she responded, "I thought you were talking to Zia. I didn't hear you say my name." Hmm...I guess it's plausible.

Which got me thinking: *Do I have Selective Hearing Syndrome with God?*

Do I conveniently tune in to God's Spirit whenever I hear Him speak words like "blessing," "healing," "prosperity," and "grace," but become deaf to words like "sacrifice," "humility," "surrender," and "accountability?" I sure hope not.

Let me take this one step further: What if God is calling you or me to do something *specific* but we aren't hearing Him? Could He (at this very moment) be calling your name without you even recognizing it?

I believe people miss God's voice for a few reasons:

1. Some are young in the Lord and they don't yet know how to recognize God's voice (like young Samuel didn't in 1 Samuel 3:4–10).

2. Some have hearts that have become calloused and hardened to His voice because of repeated disobedience to it. (Think of feet that become "numb" to walking on rocks because of repeated exposure.)

3. Some have become deaf because of spiritual pride. They do not recognize God's direction and correction through sermons, daily devotions, or other people because they are always thinking about someone else whom the message must be for. Their response is much like my daughter's: *"I thought you were talking to her."* (If you are thinking of who else needs to hear this besides yourself, you may need to be examined for Selective Hearing Syndrome!)

Whatever the reason for our selective hearing, we need to be proactive to resolve it! Much of what we are praying, asking, and believing for is contingent on our "tuning in" and obeying what God is already speaking. Maybe God has already been speaking to us, giving us specific instructions, guidance, or correction, but we have not heard Him because we don't like His counsel.

Hebrews 4:7b (NASB, emphasis added) says, *"Today, if you will hear His voice, harden not your hearts."* Notice that listening is actually optional. Notice also that it says, "Today." Right now, *today*, He is longing to speak to *you*! Resist the temptation to think that your quiet time devotion must be for Sister So-and-So or Brother Whose-a-What and instead ask God, *"What are You trying to teach me?"* He is calling you by name. And if we will still ourselves, lean in, and listen up, He will be faithful to His end of the conversation.

> *But now, thus says the Lord, He who created you, O Jacob, He who formed you, O Israel: "Fear not, for I have redeemed you; I have called you by name, you are Mine.* (Isaiah 43:1, ESV)

## TODAY'S ACTION STEP

Can you hear the voice of the Father? Take time to be still before the Lord this morning. Really listen. What did God speak to you through today's devotion? Are there any areas in your life in which you have resisted or ignored God's instruction? Ask Him to reveal to you any places of disobedience to His Word. Make the decision to follow through with any practical steps toward obedience He may reveal to you.

# DAY 19.
# Shoo Fly!

## How to Handle Temptation: Part 1

*No temptation has overtaken you but such as is common to man; and God is faithful, who will not allow you to be tempted beyond what you are able, but with the temptation will provide the way of escape also, so that you will be able to endure it.*
1 Corinthians 10:13 (NASB)

Have you ever had a fly in the room that almost drove you insane? This happened to me the other night. I think the fly was intentionally trying to aggravate me. That little demon followed me into every room! Thankfully, my husband has lightning-fast "Mr. Miyagi hands." He can catch flies with his bare hands and give them a quick and painless death. So after about thirty minutes of playing cat and mouse with Mr. Fly, I decided to call in reinforcements and appeal to my better half. He trapped that little booger in the bathroom, and we had fly soup for dinner. Mu-ah-ha-ha! (I'm kidding about the soup.)

I think temptation can often be like an annoying fly that just won't go away. Familiar sin (areas of failure we have "a history" with, or have struggled with for long seasons) has a way of pestering us, hovering over us, flitting about in front of our eyes and in our minds. It can often seem inescapable.

Even while we are trying to do our best to deny our carnal cravings, we are often aware of temptation's nagging presence as we go about our day. The pull to be drawn to things that hurt our relationship with God can follow us into any environment (yes, even into church). This can be not only frustrating but also downright depressing. Even when we experience victory over sin for a season, temptation can find its way back in when it is least expected, buzzing about relentlessly.

If you have ever felt discouraged by your struggle against sin, you are not alone. Satan is a master of custom-tailored temptation. He knows how to set us up! He can often find and exploit our weaknesses faster than we are able to even realize what is going on. Like an irritating fly, Satan uses temptation to follow us wherever we go. He capitalizes on our weakest moments, going through great strides to ensure we don't see lasting victory. Even the apostle Paul related to this struggle when he wrote in Romans 7:21–24 (NLT): *"I have discovered this principle of life—that when I want to do what is right, I inevitably do what is wrong. I love God's law with all my heart. But there is another power within me that is at war with my mind. This power makes me a slave to the sin that is still within me. Oh, what a miserable person I am! Who will free me from this life that is dominated by sin and death?"*

So, how on earth can we (once and for all) put to death the temptation that is following us around? In today and tomorrow's devotions, we will cover six steps to overcome temptation. Let's begin.

1. **Realize that temptation itself is *not* a sin.** It is not a sin to have a wrong thought pop in your head or to experience a pull toward something you shouldn't. Many people suffer from unnecessary guilt because they misunderstand this. Temptation only *becomes sin* when you let that thought stay there. (I have heard it said that "You cannot help it if a bird flies over your head, but you can stop the bird from making a nest in your hair!")

Being tempted also does not mean that you are a horrible person or that you were never saved. It is only evidence that you still have a flawed nature and you live in a broken world. We know that temptation itself is not a sin, because even Jesus was tempted! As a matter of fact, Scripture tells us that Jesus was tempted in <u>every way</u> and yet He never sinned (Hebrews 4:15). This should encourage us, to know that our High Priest knows how we feel. He is not some far-off, aloof God, testing us and waiting for us to stumble. On the contrary, He can sympathize with our weaknesses, because He has felt the weight and the struggle of temptation Himself. This is the reason He is so slow to anger, so compassionate and eager to forgive us: because He is mindful of our frame and knows we are "but dust" (see Psalm 103:14). Today, you can rejoice that you have a Savior who has *been there* and who is *still* right there with you in the midst of every temptation you face!

2.      **Realize that we all face temptation.** The words of 1 Corinthians 10:13 should be posted all over your house if you are currently struggling with temptation. Read it, memorize it, and apply it! In it, we find out that *"no temptation has overtaken us, but such as is <u>common to man</u>"* (NASB, emphasis added). Don't incorrectly assume that you are somehow worse than others because of your struggles. Friend, we ALL face times of heavy, oppressive temptation. Every one of us! We all have extremely weak moments when we genuinely, flat-out just WANT that sin! It is dangerous to isolate yourself by assuming you have it worse than the rest of your brothers and sisters in Christ. If you fail to understand that what you are going through is "common to man," you will never seek accountability or other help for fear that you are somehow defective and/or unable to overcome.

3.      **Be honest with yourself and others.** Likely the most critical mistake you can make in your struggle against sin is rationalization. Rationalization begins when you fail to take ownership of your desire to stay in sin. Oftentimes, the brutal but honest truth is that we continue to struggle with temptation because we like our sin too much to do what we need to do to get

out of it. We downplay sin's role in our lives, both to ourselves and to those who could help us walk victoriously.

While everyone is tempted in some way, the strength and duration of the temptation we experience largely lies in our willingness to face the cold, hard truth. James 1:14–15 (NLT) says, *"Temptation comes from our own desires, which entice us and drag us away. These desires give birth to sinful actions. And when sin is allowed to grow, it gives birth to death."* There is too much at stake to hide our heads in the sand and pretend we aren't struggling! Don't allow sin "to grow" and bring death as its inevitable result.

Once we stop rationalizing and confront our sin head-on, we should do two things: confess it to God and to others. First John 1:9 (NLT) says, *"But if we confess our sins to him, He is faithful and just to forgive us our sins and to cleanse us from all wickedness."* Confessing our sin to God results in forgiveness. But there's another (often missing piece) to this formula. While 1 John talks about confession to God for forgiveness, James 5:16 (NLT) says that confession to our fellow man results in healing: *"Confess your sins to each other and pray for each other so that you may be healed."*

I know it might seem humiliating, but honest confession of sin to a spouse, pastor, or parent (someone you trust) can result in the biggest breakthrough that you have ever experienced. Sin dies in the light. When we bring honest truth into our darkest areas, the light scatters the darkness away.

Tomorrow, we will finish looking at the final steps to overcome temptation. Due to the weightiness of today's topic, I want to stop and let what we have learned have a chance to marinate. Be sure to take time to go through today's action step so that you can unpack these concepts in your heart and in your life.

The buzzing of temptation stands no chance against the weight of God's Word. Like a holy flyswatter, His truth can squash the lies of the enemy once and for all! God *can and will* bring you through your trial if you will apply these biblical truths to your life.

## TODAY'S ACTION STEP

Shoo fly! Perhaps you are tired of dealing with the same areas of sin. I pray today and tomorrow, you will follow through with the difficult, but necessary steps to handling temptation. Take time to really reflect on what we have learned. How does it feel to know that temptation itself is not a sin? Does this change your ability to open up to others about what you are going through?

Before ending your quiet time, take out a journal and begin to write down any current areas of struggle. Be honest. Have you made any excuses or downplayed any sin in your life? Ask the Lord to examine your heart and reveal any possible areas of compromise or rationalization. Take time to confess to God the hidden motives of your heart; *He knows them anyway.*

Next, begin to think of someone to whom you can confess your areas of struggle. If you are married, this should be your spouse. If you are a teenager or a young adult, this should be a parent. If you feel you do not have someone with whom you can be brutally honest, consider a leader in your church of the same sex, or a strong Christian friend. Take the leap TODAY (before the enemy can talk you out of it) and set up a time to meet with that person to discuss your areas of struggle.

# DAY 20.
# Shoo Fly!

## How to Handle Temptation: Part 2

*No temptation has overtaken you but such as is common to man; and God is faithful, who will not allow you to be tempted beyond what you are able, but with the temptation will provide the way of escape also, so that you will be able to endure it.*
1 Corinthians 10:13 (NASB)

Yesterday, we discussed the first three steps to overcome temptation. Before we dive back in, be sure you have followed through with yesterday's action step. These steps are progressive and dependent upon one another. Do not try to microwave this process! If you truly desire to be rid of the pesky, disgusting fly of temptation and the destructive patterns of sin, radical change and follow-through are imperative.

Remember that Scripture says, *"Humble yourselves before God. Resist the devil, and he will flee from you"* (James 4:7, NLT). It is possible not only to rid yourself of this temptation, but it is possible to even cause the enemy to RUN from you! However, the ball is in your court (or perhaps I should say, "the flyswatter is your hand"). Your determination to humble yourself, resist Satan, and submit to the process of obedience to God's Word will determine your level of victory.

Let's continue with our steps to overcome temptation. We will pick back up at step four.

**4.** **Look for the door of escape.** The end of 1 Corinthians 10:13 tells us that God has provided what I like to call an "escape hatch" to use during times of temptation. He assures us that this way out is the reason we will always have the option to get out of the trap of sin. We will never be able to justify or rationalize our sin before a faithful God who has promised that He would never give us any temptation beyond our ability to endure it. That escape hatch is KEY to overcoming! God promises that every single temptation has been equipped with one. But like any well-placed escape hatch, you have to look for it.

Remember when Potiphar's wife tempted Joseph back in the book of Genesis? This woman was brazen, seductively dressed, and likely highly attractive. What was Joseph's response to her enticements? He RAN! Too often, we flirt with sin rather than run away from it. We play on the fence instead of looking around for a way out. We ask how much we can get away with before it's "technically" sin, when we should instead be grieved at even going near the fence because of how much it hurts God's heart!

Rather than seeing how close we can get to the edge without going over, we should be increasing our buffer zones. We should be closing every door of provision for future sin. Practically speaking, if you struggle with alcoholism, don't EVER go to parties where there is alcohol! Yes, I said it. Don't keep it in your house. Don't flirt with it. RUN! If you struggle with pornography (as more and more women are), take the Internet off of your phone and put a strong filter on your computers. You shouldn't even have social media accounts or anything that will lure you back in. If you are being drawn in by an inappropriate relationship, block the person's number and tell your spouse or another spiritual leader. Stop arranging to be where that person is. Flee from that destructive temptation!

Some may say that these measures seem extreme, but those same people are most often the ones who live their lives defeated by sin. You will undoubtedly have bad days. You will have guaranteed weak moments, but if you have already burned your bridges, it will become harder to fall on those days. Stop making provisions for your future self to sin! That is what you are doing when you ignore that still, small voice of conviction and knowingly stay too close to the line of sin. When you are tempted, RUN! Again, tell someone you trust to pray for you and confess the temptation to them. Remember, sin dies in the light but it feeds on darkness. Ask God for the door of escape (i.e., leave that place of temptation and go somewhere else immediately), and then take it.

5. **Learn the art of replacement versus simple denial.** We should handle temptation the way Jesus did: with the Word of God. Instead of just simply denying yourself, begin to pray and speak God's Word when you are tempted.

Christianity is not behavior modification. You can't overcome sin on your own! You need Jesus. You need to wield the sword of God's Word. Ephesians 6:17 (NLT) says, *"And take the sword of the Spirit, which is the word of God."* God's Word is an incredibly powerful offensive weapon against the strategies of the enemy. Hebrews 4:12 (NLT) gives us a glimpse of how strong this weapon is: *"For the word of God is alive and powerful. It is sharper than the sharpest two-edged sword, cutting between soul and spirit, between joint and marrow. It exposes our innermost thoughts and desires."*

Instead of simply repressing urges, find scriptures that speak to your struggle. Screenshot them. Write them on your mirror in lipstick. Post them on stickie notes in your car. Confess them when you are facing temptation. This will actually have a backfire effect on the enemy because it will draw you closer to the Word and to Christ. Every time Satan tempts you, begin to worship, begin to pray, and begin to confess God's Word. Eventually, Satan will realize He is actually drawing you toward Christ, and he will quit messing with you! He will FLEE from you!

6. **Realize that if you are a child of God, you are already free from sin.** Bottom line: If you have given your life to Jesus, the power to be victorious is already in your hands. Sin and death

have already been defeated. Christ stripped sin of its power and handed you that victory the day you gave your life to Him. The only power Satan has over you is the power you willingly give to him. Don't do it. Don't allow him to convince you that he is the one with the upper hand.

Romans 6:6 (NLT) says, *"We know that our old sinful selves were crucified with Christ so that sin might lose its power in our lives. We are no longer slaves to sin."* Sin can only control you if you hand over the reins of your heart and allow it to. Christ paid too high of a price for your freedom for you to allow the enemy to be in the driver's seat of your life. Stand up to him, resist him with the truth, and hold him accountable to the fact that, as a joint-heir with Jesus, YOU are the one who is victorious!

Friends, the tempter's voice becomes stronger every time you let it control you. Conversely, each time you resist the temptation by running away from it and running toward Christ, sin weakens its grip on you. If you want the fly of temptation to go away, RESIST IT! On those days when that stupid fly has driven you to the point of a breakdown, remember who is greater! Begin to cry out to your Savior, who can sympathize with your weaknesses because He's been there. He paid the price to set you free and He has not left you to fight the battle defenseless. He has the power to whip out His divine "Mr. Miyagi hands" and put that temptation where it belongs: under your feet!

## TODAY'S ACTION STEP

Ask God to reveal to you any areas where you may be "making provision for the flesh" or leaving doors open for future sin. Take out your journal. Write down any ways you can close doors or run from temptation. What is your escape hatch?

Do a topical search today on scriptures that speak to your particular struggle. *(For example: Google "scriptures on fear" or "scriptures on lust," or do a word search on biblegateway.com or through a Bible app).* Write down the verses that most speak to you (or screenshot them) and post them around your house. Commit to memorizing one or two this week; hide God's Word in your heart so that you might not sin against Him (see Psalm 119:11). Finally, practice reading or reciting these verses every time you are tempted to sin.

# DAY 21.
# Benjamin Button Christianity

*For apart from me you can do nothing.*
John 15:5 (NLT)

You may have heard of a movie produced several years ago titled "The Curious Case of Benjamin Button." It was loosely based on a 1922 short story about a boy named Benjamin who aged in reverse. In the short story, the boy was born able to talk and had the appearance of an old man. As he "grew up," Benjamin actually became younger and younger. After oddly aging backward and hitting every milestone in reverse, Benjamin eventually died with the mental capacity and function of a newborn, aware only of his nurse.

Weird. (*Insert cricket chirp and awkward pause.*)

A-hem. Anyway, the story is bizarre, but it inspired me to write a bit about what I call "Benjamin Button Christianity."

Let me explain.

In the natural world, the more we mature, the more <u>independent</u> we become. When we are first born, we are completely reliant on others for our survival. Yet, as we grow up, we become more self-sufficient. We (hopefully) no longer need help providing ourselves with food, clothes, and/or using the bathroom.

In the supernatural world, the more we mature, the more <u>dependent</u> we become. As a matter of fact, I believe the hallmark of a mature Christian is a curious and complete dependency on

God. As we grow in Christ and His Word, we realize we no longer can depend on our own wisdom, charisma, wit, or skill. We come to understand that "apart from Christ, we can do nothing" (see John 15:55).

In John 21:18–19 (NLT), Jesus rocked Peter's world with this statement: "*I tell you the truth, when you were young, you were able to do as you liked; you dressed yourself and went wherever you wanted to go. But when you are old, you will stretch out your hands, and others will dress you and take you where you don't want to go." Jesus said this to let* Peter *know by what kind of death he would ultimately glorify God. Then Jesus told him, "Follow me."*

Jesus correctly prophesied that Peter would unquestionably relinquish his rights to call the shots in his own life, and subsequently, in his death. (History tells us that Peter was later martyred for his faith and crucified upside-down on a cross.)

In this profound statement to Peter, Christ alluded to the fact that <u>maturity in the Kingdom of God is paralleled with surrender</u>. An immature, selfish believer demands their own rights, but a mature, wise follower of Christ realizes that they have given complete lordship of their heart to Jesus. They have been "bought with a price," (1 Corinthians 6:20 ESV) and they no longer consider telling Christ "no" a viable option.

This systematic relinquishing of our own rights will undoubtedly rub today's independent-spirited Christian the wrong way. Especially in America, we pride ourselves on having a spirit of defiance and independence.

*I got this. I can do this all by myself.*

Yet in John 15:4–5 (NLT), Jesus said this: "*Remain in me, and I will remain in you. For a branch cannot produce fruit if it is severed from the vine, and you cannot be fruitful unless you remain in me. Yes, I am the vine; you are the branches. Those who remain in me, and I in them, will produce much fruit. For apart from me you can do nothing."*

Imagine for a moment, if you will, a branch deciding it no longer likes the vine. It decides it prefers to feel the dirt beneath it for itself. It questions the motive of the vine and wonders why it needs the vine at all. It wonders why the vine thinks it knows so much, when it's so old and outdated anyway.

So, the branch pulls out.

It drops to the ground and feels the ecstasy of freedom, once and for all. For one glorious day, it lies on the ground, uninhibited by the vine's orders and restraints. It revels in the unveiled sunlight. Granted, it can't create fruit anymore, but, hey, at least it's got its freedom!

Until a day later, when it shrivels up and dies. The end.

Weird. (*Insert cricket chirp and awkward pause.*)

This is the picture of a Christian who finds the beautiful, life-giving, sustaining power of the Word of God restrictive and imposing, and who therefore decides to go her own way. She pulls away from the only thing that can save her or help her to effortlessly bear fruit, only to end up burned, broken, and fruitless.

Jesus, the Son of the Living God, made this amazing statement in John 5:19–20a (NIV): "*I tell you the truth, the Son can do nothing by Himself. He does only what he sees the Father doing. Whatever the Father does, the Son also does. For the Father loves the Son and shows Him everything He is doing.*"

Did you catch that? The Son of God only did what He saw the Father doing! Jesus repeated this many times in His lifetime. The essence of Perfection yielded His life on earth to the will of His Father. And so should we.

So, practically speaking, who is running your life? Who calls the shots in how you operate in your marriage? Who (or what) makes financial decisions for you? Career decisions? Where do you receive parenting advice? Relationship advice?

If your answer is popular opinion, social media polls, advice from friends or your mom (Lord, bless her), celebrity opinions, your "gut," self-help books, or modern psychology, you are relying on the unreliable! The ONLY way to truly bear lasting fruit in any area of your life is through radical, complete dependency on God's Word. Rest assured, you will have every possible rationalization of why your case is different and why God's Word won't work for you. You will be tempted to pull out and claim your independence: DON'T DO IT.

God wants to give you the beautiful rest of a child again. The complete release of control produces a supernatural peace. I beg you to examine every area of your life through the lens of Scripture. If there is an area that is dysfunctional and/or not bearing fruit, discover what God's Word says about it, then do it. Relinquish your right to call the shots, connect to the Vine, and allow God's Word to bring light and life to that area again. Don't allow pride and self-reliance to bring pain for one more day.

Spiritually aging in reverse can seem as curious as the tale of Benjamin Button. It can, at first, seem frightening to release control to the Father. Yet, it ironically produces peace.

Wouldn't you like to experience the bliss of childhood again? You can. You are a child of the Most High God, and He has already given you every answer to life and godliness. It is found while abiding in His Word.

## TODAY'S ACTION STEP

Are you spiritually maturing properly? Are you becoming less self-reliant and more Word-dependent each day?

Write down any areas of your life that are not bearing good fruit. Ask the Father to show you what His Word says about that area of your life. Begin to seek His will in this situation. (If you don't know what God's Word says about your situation, do a word search through Scripture or ask a spiritual leader or friend to show you in the Bible.)

Commit to "reconnecting" with the Vine of God's Word by doing what the Word of God says consistently, in EVERY area of your life, despite the pushback from your flesh. You WILL see fruit if you continue to abide!

# DAY 22.
# The Best Blankie Ever

*I will not leave you comfortless: I will come to you.*
John 14:18 (KJV)

As babies, each of my four children had a favorite blanket. Some of them slept with these blankets until they were in elementary school. My youngest daughter is two and calls her blanket a "ganky." She takes the tag attached to it and rubs it on her cheek when she is sleepy. If you are on her good side, and she is feeling especially generous, she will even rub your cheek with her ganky tag. It is quite adorable. You rarely see her without her ganky. Something about it brings her comfort and peace, especially when she is hurting or unsure of her surroundings.

I've heard of some kids holding on to what's left of their baby blankets even into adulthood. The once-lovely blanket has been reduced to faded, worn scraps and yet they still sleep with it every night.

I don't have a childhood blankie, but I do have a favorite quilt. I have slept with it so many years in a row that it's now tattered and torn. I've tried other blankets and comforters, but this one has the magical property of being both cold and warm at the same time. It's just warm enough to snuggle up with on a brisk autumn morning, without being too hot in the summertime.

A good comforter is designed to help you rest and to bring you peace and relief after a day of hard work. It is something children grow partial to because it becomes a constant in the face of dark nights, a change in their environment, sickness, or pain.

Jesus gave us a beautiful promise in John 14:16–18 (KJV). He said, "*And I will pray the Father, and he shall give you another Comforter, that he may abide with you for ever; Even the Spirit of truth; whom the world cannot receive, because it seeth him not, neither knoweth him: but ye know him; for he dwelleth with you, and shall be in you. I will not leave you comfortless: I will come to you.*"

At the time Jesus spoke this, He was warning His disciples that His time on earth was coming to an end. He knew that He would soon ascend to heaven and leave the disciples on earth to fulfill their part of the Great Commission.

This must have been terrifying for them. They had left their homes, their jobs, and their livelihood for Jesus, and now He was speaking of leaving them.

Yet, ever compassionate and aware of their needs, Jesus spoke to their concerns. He promised not to leave them alone, but that He would send them a Comforter. A divine blankie, if you will—the Holy Spirit.

I love this thought. Regardless of how tough we pride ourselves on being, we all have moments when we become like frightened children, in need of comfort. Life has a way of bringing turmoil, pain, nerve-racking change, uneasiness, and hurt. Certain seasons can reduce us to feeling like helpless children. These times make it difficult for our souls to find rest and peace.

Cue the Holy Spirit.

Sent as a Divine Blanket during stress and anxiety, He is available to us for our every need. Jesus said, "*I am leaving you with a gift—peace of mind and heart. And the peace I give is a gift the world cannot give. So don't be troubled or afraid*" (John 14:27, NLT).

Jesus promises to give us rest when we come to Him. In Matthew 11:28–30 (NLT), He says, "*Come to me, all of you who are weary and carry heavy burdens, and I will give you rest. Take my yoke upon you. Let me teach you, because I am humble and gentle at heart, and you will find rest for your souls. For my yoke is easy to bear, and the burden I give you is light.*"

He says, "*I will not leave you as orphans; I will come to you*" (John 14:18, NLT)

How beautiful! What comfort to know that your good Daddy is close to you, regardless of what you are going through. He promises to swallow you in peace like a father scoops up a child, if you will just come to Him. The Holy Spirit is the best blankie ever, available to every son and daughter, every weary child of God.

If you are hurting or tired today, find comfort in knowing that Christ is with you. His Presence is available, and He has not left you to walk alone. Climb up in His lap, grab His comfort, and surround yourself with His sweet peace.

## TODAY'S ACTION STEP

Today, God wants to do a holy exchange: He desires to swap your anxiety for a peace that "surpasses all understanding." He promises that all we have to do is "cast our cares on Him" and He will keep us in perfect peace, if we fix our minds on Him. Take time right now (perhaps even get on your knees) and bring your cares and concerns to the Father. Let the Holy Spirit blanket you with His Presence as you listen to a worship song and ask Him to fill the room with His comfort and peace. Determine to fix your mind on the goodness and faithfulness of God.

# DAY 23.
# But FIRST, Let Me Take a #Selfie

*But seek first the kingdom of God and his righteousness, and all these things will be added to you.*
Matthew 6:33 (ESV)

We live in a selfie generation.

In case you have been living in a cave and don't know what a "selfie" is, it's a picture you take of yourself, usually for the purpose of posting on social media. You may have heard the popular phrase or viral song, "But First Let Me Take a #Selfie," which teases about our culture's narcissistic obsession with self-documentation.

There's nothing inherently wrong with taking selfies. I do it myself. But it's a pretty hilarious social experiment to sit and watch others as they try to take the perfect self-portrait. I have many times seen girls alone in their cars in a store parking lot, fixing their hair, pursing their lips, and posing over and over to capture that perfect selfie. It's pretty humorous to watch from the outside.

Some people seem like there's nothing they enjoy more than their own image. Their social media profiles are littered with their own pictures (often posting them several times a day). And while I do think you should "love the skin you're in," I have to wonder if we have perhaps crossed over the line from a healthy self-image to the flat-out worship of self. Even sadder, I believe that if we are honest, most of this compulsive selfie behavior is actually rooted in our need for validation and approval versus stemming from confidence.

Self-doubt is often the consequence of self-worship.

Don't get me wrong. I am not trying to make a light-hearted topic like selfies into something too heavy or deep. But I can't resist contrasting the title of this viral cultural song, "But First Let Me Take a #Selfie," with the use of the word "first" in Matthew 6:33. It's too obvious for me not to point out the disparity between the me-first culture of America and the God-first culture of the Bible.

> But seek first the kingdom of God and his righteousness, and all these things will be added to you. (Matthew 6:33, ESV)

One culture instructs you to "seek first the KINGDOM"; the other to "put yourself first." But what does it matter which comes first anyway?

Let's look at the definition of the word "first." A simple Google word search produces this definition:

> "Coming before all others in time or order."

> "Foremost in position, rank, or importance."

These definitions tell me that what you put first in your life determines your priorities, your schedule, your devotion—your very *worship*.

The Ten Commandments very famously state in Exodus 20:3–5 (NASB): "*You shall have no other gods before Me. You shall not make for yourself an idol, or any likeness of what is in heaven above or on the earth beneath or in the water under the earth. You shall not worship them or serve them.*"

No doubt, you probably don't make wooden idols and bow down to them. But I do believe that the people of our nation have created a god in our own image. I daily see the exaltation of "self" in America, as people bow down and worship their own desires, their own feelings and comfort, and their own preferences and ideas. We place most of our money, our attention, and our schedules down on the altar of our own convenience and pleasure. The rank and file of our hearts is often yielded to the person staring back at us—through the reverse image of the cameras on our mobile devices.

If we are really honest, we value ourselves first in time and order; we value ourselves foremost in position, rank, and importance.

But this hyper-fixation on the love of ourselves backfires. While promising confidence, it actually breeds insecurity. Instead of joy, it produces depression and self-hatred. This is because there is only One who is worthy to retain the first position in our hearts and affections. His name is Jesus. He is seated unrivaled in heaven, and He should similarly be unrivaled on the thrones of our hearts.

He should be our first thought when we wake up. He alone should call the shots in our lives, pulling rank when our stubborn flesh wants to go its own way. He should not receive stale, leftover devotion.

*"I didn't have time to read my Bible today."*
*"Unless I have something else I want or need to do, I will be at church on Sunday."*
*"I'll tithe when I get a raise, God, I need the money now."*
*"Sundays are my only day to sleep in."*
*"I'm just too busy to serve in church."*
*"I don't feel like getting up to have my quiet time with God. I'm too tired."*

These are the mantras of self-worship. God doesn't want some of you; He wants *all* of you. God doesn't want a piece of your heart; He wants *all* of it. God deserves our first and our best. Just ask Cain. He thought he could get by with a substandard offering to the Lord, unlike his brother Abel's first and best.

> *Cain presented some of his crops as a gift to the Lord. Abel also brought a gift—the best portions of the firstborn lambs from his flock. The Lord accepted Abel and his gift, but He did not accept Cain and his gift.* (Genesis 4:3b–5a, NLT)

It has been said, "If you give God your first and best, He will bless the rest." If you, by faith and obedience to the God who purchased your heart with the blood of His Son, determine to keep Him seated first in rank and priority in your life, He will "add all these things," as His Word promises.

Don't put the cart before the horse. Instead, put first things first and then watch how the things that others chase down will actually chase YOU down. Deuteronomy 28:2 (ESV) promises, "*And all these blessings shall come upon you and overtake you, if you obey the voice of the Lord your God.*"

I have seen this countless times in my own life and the lives of those around me. I watch others strive for things that I don't even ask God for and receive. It is not because I am special. It is because it has been promised that if I seek first God's Kingdom, then "all these things will be added." This very same promise has been given to you. The blessings and rewards, the peace and joy, the things for which others spin their wheels, bankrupt their families, and waste their days trying to pursue, will actually pursue you—if you seek Him first.

## TODAY'S ACTION STEP

Is God truly first in your life? Take time to pray and ask God to reveal any areas in which you may have dethroned Jesus or offered Him your second best. This week, practice giving God your first every morning. Before you look at your phone and/or answer any text messages, before you get dressed, become still before the Father. Give Him all of your "firsts." Make a commitment to give God the first day of your week by being faithful in the house of God. Commit to honoring Him with the firstfruits of your finances by being faithful to tithe (the word "tithe" means ten percent) to your local church. These steps are a matter of faith and trust in God's Word versus your own understanding. If you "keep them with all diligence," you will soon begin to see tangible evidence of the favor of God.

# DAY 24.
# Cooking Up a Plan to Sin

*But put ye on the Lord Jesus Christ, and make not provision for the flesh, to* fulfill *the lusts* thereof.
Romans 13:14 (KJV)

I'm a planner, a strategizer. I like to think ahead. I like to dream big, bold ideas and then overcome obstacles to make those ridiculously larger-than-life ideas come to fruition.

This attribute can be good when it comes to certain things: leading a women's ministry, planting a church, even planning a meal with a scarce pantry. I have cooked up quite the creative meal in my day from almost nothing!

But determination and strategy can also be a bad thing at times. In my broken, scarred past, I have fallen victim more than once to strategizing a way to let my flesh have its fix for its carnal cravings. I have gone out of my way to sin, I have disobeyed God's Word, and I have hurled myself headlong into a path of destruction. If not for God's redeeming grace and mercy, I would be dead because of my flesh's creative skill at accomplishing its own stubborn will.

I came across a provoking scripture today: Romans 13:14 (KJV) says, "*But put ye on the Lord Jesus Christ, and make not provision for the flesh, to fulfill the lusts thereof.*"

When I looked up this phrase in Strong's Concordance in the original Greek, I found that it can be translated this way: "*And do not construct, form, fashion or produce any forethought or providential care for the flesh, to fulfill its cravings, longings, desires."*

I believe that one of the first steps in overcoming destructive patterns of sin is to acknowledge that we have done more than just "sin." Usually we have actually devised ways to accomplish that sin after hours of thinking about it, ruminating over it, and meditating on it. Sin is ALWAYS born from our thought life. What we think is fantasy is more likely strategy.

If we truly want to stop falling into the same areas of temptation, then we must be honest with ourselves at the embryonic stages of sin—our thought life. We must acknowledge before God that our sin was not a haphazard mistake, but rather a thought-out, meticulously strategized plan to disobey. Then we must CUT, SEVER, and BURN any bridge that would ever allow us to go back down that road. Whether we care to admit it or not, as long as we leave an open door for sin in our lives, we are making provision or providential care for that sin at a future time. When we flirt with sin, we will soon find ourselves married to it!

Do you TRULY want to be free, once and for all, from life-dominating sins? Christ has already set you free. Now it is your choice to burn some bridges. Make it nearly impossible for yourself to fall in a weak moment. Block that number, delete that account, confess your addiction or inappropriate relationship to your spouse, talk to your doctor about your addiction to pain medication. Do whatever you need to do to cut off the provision you have subconsciously made for future sin. Have the courage to be honest with yourself about the sin that you have nurtured in the dark.

You can be free, and free indeed, through Christ. The choice is yours! Go ahead and cancel plans with tomorrow's sin. That's a date you can't afford to keep.

## TODAY'S ACTION STEP

Are you cooking up a plan to sin? Thus far on our journey, we have attempted to pinpoint areas of compromise. You may have even made some progress in certain areas. The Arise Phase is about action! It's time to get serious and make some big changes by burning any bridges that would lead you back down the wrong path. Have the courage to take some of the previously suggested action steps this week to ensure your continual freedom.

# DAY 25.
# My Knees Are Hurting!

*So let's not get tired of doing what is good. At just the right time
we will reap a harvest of blessing if we don't give up.*
Galatians 6:9 (NLT)

All three of my daughters are fiercely independent. Each of them
came out of the womb wanting to do things all on their own. At
year one, they each insisted on spoon-feeding themselves. As
early as fifteen months, they each fought me to dress themselves
unassisted. Getting out the door with a four-year-old who
maintains that she needs no help tying her shoes or buttoning her
jacket can be quite painful! These girls of mine, they want to do it
*all on their own.*

My boy? Not so much.

My son, Elias, is now six years old, and he could not be more
different from his sisters. He has always been content for me to
completely feed him, dress him, and even (*ahem*) wipe him since
birth. At three, he would pretend his hands were limp and insist
that I needed to spoon-feed him. For a very long time, I thought
something was actually wrong with his legs, because when he
would walk, he would cry and say, "My knees are hurting! I can't
walk!" But after having him repeatedly checked by our
pediatrician, we learned that physically he is fine. He simply
prefers to let me carry his giant self as we walk around the mall.
With no shortage of women in the family to baby him, we have

finally had to insist that he begin to walk, feed, and (*ahem*) wipe himself on his own, whether he feels like it or not.

Generally speaking, I don't give in to his whining. But he *IS* my only boy. So, occasionally, I do baby him and hold him or tie his shoes (even though he's perfectly capable of doing it himself). I can't help it. He's my baby. When he looks at me and says, "*Girl, you so beautiful and holy,*" as he does nearly every day, I'm pretty much putty in his hands.

But for the most part, Elias has had to adapt to the fact that he must do things for himself even when he's tired or doesn't feel like it. It's a part of growing up. I'm pretty sure his future wife wouldn't appreciate it if I continued to do these things for him. It would make for one awkward honeymoon someday!

Nevertheless, I do feel compassion for the little dude. Sometimes life is tiring. Our hands get weak, and our knees get feeble. We become unsure whether we can continue on— especially on what can be an intense and soul-searching journey like this one. We can get "weary of well doing."

Today I want to encourage you to press on. Hebrews 12:11–13 (NLT) says, "*No discipline is enjoyable while it is happening—it's painful! But afterward there will be a peaceful harvest of right living for those who are trained in this way. So, take a new grip with your tired hands and strengthen your weak knees. Mark out a straight path for your feet so that those who are weak and lame will not fall but become strong.*"

Are your "knees hurting?" Are you tired today? The compassion of a mother would love to scoop you up and carry you through this, to do it all for you. But God is training you through the pain. He is equipping you through the process. Like a holy boot camp instructor, your Daddy God is making your arms strong for this task, even when you feel you can't bear any more weight.

Proverbs 31:17 (ESV) says that the virtuous woman *"dresses herself with strength and makes her arms strong."* So today, my sweet sister, don't become weary in well doing. You WILL reap, if you faint not. This process will produce beauty on the other side of the pain. Take a new grip. (Yes, God's Word just said to "get a grip.") Strengthen those weak knees. Mark out a straight path. You can do this through the power of His Spirit!

I am praying for you today to have renewed strength as you wait before the Father. Holy Spirit, I ask for supernatural energy and enthusiasm in your girl—for a holy shot of vitamin B12 to help your daughter see this process through to completion, in Jesus' name!

## TODAY'S ACTION STEP

We all get weak kneed and weary at times. Today, encourage yourself in the Lord by reading these passages of Scripture: Psalm 27:14; Isaiah 40:31; and Matthew 11:28–30. Did you notice the prescription given for weariness and fatigue? Try the Word's holy remedy for spiritual exhaustion and allow the Lord to meet you at your point of need.

# DAY 26.
# My Quite Un-fabulous Today

*God has made everything beautiful for its own time.*
Ecclesiastes 3:11a (NLT)

"Mommy, I am the queen of Weff Birginia [West Virginia]," my five-year-old daughter proclaimed. "Oh, really?" I asked. "Yes! And Daddy is the king," she continued proudly. "Eden is the princess, and Elias is the prince. And you, Mommy—you are the maid."

*Gee, thanks.*

I chuckled, but honestly, I felt like there was some truth to what she had just said. Sometimes I *do* feel like a maid! There has been more than one occasion when I felt small and insignificant in the scheme of eternity, like Rosie, the robot maid on the cartoon series The Jetsons.

Sometimes *real* life can be *really* unglamorous. Covered in baby vomit, and contending with diapers and spaghetti noodles as you re-mop the floor you *just* mopped. Redoing a homework assignment for school because the computer crashed and you lost the paper you already wrote. This is what real life looks like.

Chores. Errands. Work. Spreadsheets. Papers. Dirty socks. Old milk bottles found encrusted under the backseats of your SUV. (*God only knows how long THAT was under there!*)

So we escape from the reality of school, our jobs, and housework for a moment to scroll through social media. BAD IDEA.

*"Oh, Ashley just got a new house and it looks like it should be featured on HGTV."*
*"Oh, Megan is six weeks' postpartum and already has a six-pack."*
*"Oh, Katie's husband surprised her with an impromptu trip to Hawaii."*
*"Oh, Samantha just got featured on the cover of 'People' magazine for saving the world with her bionic hair."* (Okay, maybe that was a bit too much, but you get my drift!)

If you are like me at all, sometimes you feel like you are trapped inside the mundane. You may have imagined that you would be living your dreams by now, but instead you find yourself a prisoner in Diaper Dungeon.

It's easy to feel as though your small, daily tasks are insignificant. But this way of thinking is also dangerous. It's not surprising that we are tempted to trivialize normalcy. Scripture makes it clear that "*if you are faithful in little things, you will be faithful in large ones*" (Luke 16:10a, NLT).

I believe very strongly that "fixation on the fabulous" is hazardous to a targeted, purpose-filled life. Satan is well aware that you cannot be any good in *this season* if he can keep you longing for *another* one.

So the enemy belittles what God sees as beautiful: the small things. He instigates an unholy preoccupation with an exciting, glamorous life.

If we aren't careful, this quickly leads to coveting what we don't have: someone else's home, someone else's job, someone else's husband. *Yep, I just went there.* This selfish, distracted road will lead to inattention to our own homes, our own husbands, our own kids, or our own schoolwork. The pursuit of "something more" will inevitably lead to negligence in the very things that God has called us to do, the very places that will launch us into our destinies.

The virtuous woman in Proverbs 31 has been long held up in Christianity as a model to follow. But if this chapter is read in its entirety, you will find something curiously overlooked: a normal, everyday life.

My pastor's wife once pointed out to me that out of all the twenty-one verses describing the virtuous woman, only one is about community outreach. The other twenty verses describe the work she does in her own home, serving her own children and her own husband. This famous chapter of the Bible exalts normalcy over the glam. It finds beauty in the behind-the-scenes sacrifices of a mom and a wife.

The Bible calls noble what our culture condemns as menial.

I feel obligated to encourage you not to get so distracted (even with hyper-spiritual tasks) that you neglect your daily responsibilities. Your calling in life hinges on your faithfulness in the small things, especially the things that no one else wants to do. I have been mandated to share this with you!

Titus 2:4–5 (NLT) states very clearly: "*These older women must train the younger women to love their husbands and their children, to live wisely and be pure, to work in their homes, to do good, and to be submissive to their husbands. Then they will not bring shame on the word of God.*"

The "other woman" described in the book of Proverbs (the wayward, promiscuous type) is not found in the home. She is out chasing other things, coveting another life, one more sophisticated and exciting than the one she has been given.

*Then out came a woman to meet him, dressed like a prostitute and with crafty intent. (She is unruly and defiant, her feet never stay at home; now in the street, now in the squares, at every corner she lurks.)* (Proverbs 7:10–12, NIV)

This distracted life gives birth to disillusionment. It breeds vanity and depression, jealousy and greed. It will blind you from the satisfaction that only a hard day's work can bring. It robs you of the rewards produced from difficult tasks being done to completion in love and in service of others. Tragically, it pulls you off the only path that leads to abundant life. It makes you wayward, ignorant, and unfruitful in what really matters.

> *She (the wayward woman) gives no thought to the way of life; her paths wander aimlessly, but she does not know it.* (Proverbs 5:6, NIV)

In a society obsessed with the rich and famous, our measure of success is so incredibly different from God's. God does not care about what man thinks deserves applause. As a matter of fact, He so loves modest, humble beginnings that He wrapped His only Son in normalcy when He showed up two thousand years ago, born in a barn to a carpenter and a teenage girl.

Scripture even tells us that Jesus' physical appearance here on earth wasn't all that glamorous: *"There was nothing beautiful or majestic about his appearance, nothing to attract us to him"* (Isaiah 53:2b, NLT). I don't know about you, but if I had been in charge of designing my own face, I would have made myself look "hawwwt!" But not Jesus—He modeled humility in every way.

He lived His life from the manger to the cross in complete service to those who could never repay Him. He bent down to love the helpless, eat dinner with the scorned, and wash the feet of His betrayers. Christ faithfully obeyed His Father in each season: whether it was in raising the dead or submitting to His mother, Mary. He was as faithful submitting to the parents He had created in His own grandmothers' wombs (*think about THAT for a second!*) as He was in laying His holy life down for you and me. He did not reject the little things; He embraced them—and so should we.

Colossians 3:23 (NLT) commands, *"Work willingly at whatever you do, as though you were working for the Lord rather than for people."* First Timothy 4:15 (NLT) says, *"Give your complete attention to these matters. Throw yourself into your tasks so that everyone will see your progress."*

Ecclesiastes 3:11 (NLT) says, *"God has made everything beautiful for its own time. He has planted eternity in the human heart, but even so, people cannot see the whole scope of God's work from beginning to end."*

Let us not miss the beauty in our own season!

I have determined that if Christ was okay with being a servant, I should be okay with being a mom or a grandmother, a student or a businesswoman, yes, even a maid. I'll let others wear the crowns of royalty, and I'll find contentment in washing little feet.

God, help us to see Your work from its beginning to its end. Help us to "stay at home," where You have planted us, and not rush after a day that has not yet come. Keep us from looking back with regret, remorseful at having missed important moments. Help us to be present and faithful with today so that we can eat the fruits of it tomorrow.

## TODAY'S ACTION STEP

Take time to read Proverbs 31, especially verses 20–31. Write down the things that stick out most to you. Notice how hardworking and faithful the virtuous woman is to what some may say are menial tasks. Are there any quite "un-fabulous" areas of your life that you are neglecting? Take time to repent of any selfishness in this area. Ask God to give you renewed passion for each and every task with which He has entrusted you. Determine to "turn work into worship" by throwing yourself into your daily tasks, doing them all "as unto the Lord."

# DAY 27.
# The Five-Minute Warning

*No man, having put his hand to the plough, and looking back, is*
*fit for the kingdom of God.*
Luke 9:62 (KJV)

All four of my children inherited the super-social gene from their mother. Every one of them loves to be around other people. And it's a good thing they do! We pastor a large church, so we are frequently in others' homes and at events with big crowds.

While some parents may struggle to get their children to stay around other people, I seem to have the opposite problem. When we visit places (especially places that have other children there also), my kids never want to leave. For me, the most draining part of taking our four kids out is the exit plan. Rounding up all four of my children and their stuff is like herding cats, complete with large amounts of moaning and whining over not wanting to leave.

To help combat this issue, I have learned to implement the "five-minute warning." I use this parenting technique to prepare my kids for our departure and to make it easier for them to leave social fun zones. With a five-minute heads-up, they won't be so surprised when we suddenly have to leave. It has been designed by parenting gurus to help a mama out.

Almost six years ago, when we first left our home in Louisiana to plant a church in West Virginia, God gave me a hard lesson through a story in Luke 9. Here, Christ was speaking with a couple of men who wanted to become His disciples and follow

Him. Feeling the call from Jesus, these men made two requests: *"Lord, suffer me first to go and bury my father"* (verse 59, KJV), and *"Lord, I will follow thee, but first let me go bid [my family] farewell"* (verse 61, KJV). To me, these seem like two valid requests. These men weren't asking to go get one more mocha frappe or to make a quick stop at the mall. They were asking to attend to a basic need for closure with their families; they wanted to savor one last moment with what they were leaving behind.

Yet Jesus replied, *"Let the dead bury their dead; but go thou and preach the kingdom of God.... No man, having put his hand to the plough, and looking back, is fit for the kingdom of God"* (verses 60, 62, KJV).

Wow. Isn't that a little harsh, Jesus?

When Jesus made this statement, He was alluding to a word picture. In those days, farmers would stand behind an ox that was harnessed to a plow. The responsibility of the farmer would be to encourage the ox forward, and while doing so, to keep the row straight. The farmers would keep the rows straight by picking an object (such as a tree) in the distance and focusing intently on that landmark while plowing ahead. If the farmer were to get distracted by something to the right or the left or (even worse) by something behind them, the rows would begin to suffer the consequences, as they would become crooked.

I very vividly remember sitting in a Birmingham hotel on what was our last stop on the way to our new home in West Virginia. We had heard God's emphatic call to plant a church back in my husband's hometown. We were excited beyond measure at the task with which God had entrusted us. Yet the weeks leading up to the big move had been a very painful five-minute warning from God. There were lots of tearful good-byes to family and friends. There was a death to the only life I had ever known. There was a decision to follow God, even when my desire was to stay back behind with those I loved.

There have been many moments when I was tempted to turn back. Especially during the first year of our move, there was a great temptation to return to the familiar, easier place. I remember many times having to stay off of social media completely, for fear that I would return to my old home in my heart and be unable to pour myself completely into my new task. This was hard! Missing the birth of my nephew, my son having his first birthday without his grandparents, and watching my children hurt over absent loved ones and friends was painful. There were lots of tears. Some days there still are.

But as much as I love my family, I love my Savior more.

There was, and still is, work to be done. Mentally, emotionally, spiritually, and physically, I have had to choose to leave that phase of my life and not look back. My face has to be set like a flint on the Author and Perfector of my faith and the work He has placed in my hands. This work is too important for me to allow any crooked rows. I have had to consciously decide to look ahead and not behind. I have had to die to my old life and completely embrace the new life God has given me.

Maybe throughout this journey, you sense God is bringing you to a new place, asking you to enter a new season, or take on a new task. Maybe, even now, you sense a holy five-minute warning. Resist the urge to go into it kicking and screaming. Go willingly where God asks you to go.

And, once you take that step of faith, fight the temptation to look longingly in the rearview mirror at what you are leaving behind. I have seen many, many people set out to do a God-work, only to make a U-turn because of emotional ties they were unable to break. Hebrews 11:15 (NLT) says, *"If they had been thinking of the country they had left, they would have had opportunity to return."* The truth is, we will most often find our feet moving where we allow our hearts to go.

Friend, while what you are leaving behind may have been a beautiful and God-ordained season, you cannot be effective at where you are now if you are constantly longing to be where you were back then. The rows we are plowing right now aren't just for us. They are for those who will come behind us.

So, say good-bye to the old season; let go, look on, and plow ahead. *It will be worth it one day.*

## TODAY'S ACTION STEP

Take out your journal and begin to write down any areas in your life in which you may sense God's five-minute warning. Are there seasons or tasks that God may be bringing to a close? Take time to ask yourself whether there is anyone or anything tempting you to be drawn away from radical obedience to Christ.

If you have recently made a hard decision or taken a challenging step of faith, have you been tempted to look back? If so, take practical steps to set your gaze straight ahead once again (like fasting from social media or refraining from daydreaming about your old life).

# THE SHINE PHASE

*Awake, sleeper, and arise from the dead, And*
***Christ will shine on you****.*
Ephesians 5:14 (NASB)

Wow, we have come so far! It's time for the final phase of our journey: the Shine Phase. We will now begin to shift from receiving our personal victory over bondage to experiencing the empowerment we need to use our journeys for eternal purposes. God awakens us for a purpose: to shine as a beacon of hope for others who are hurting. Our focus will change during this final stage to one of "others-ness," in which we will see that we were meant to live for more than just ourselves, and that God has a job for us to do while we are here on the earth. It is in this final stage that we will begin to find the joy that comes from living life with an eternal, Kingdom-focused perspective.

Congratulations on finishing the first two phases of the ARISE Journey! Before moving on, take time to watch a special message from the author by visiting arisejourney.com/phasethree.

# DAY 28.
# Holy Bling

*They will sparkle in his land like jewels in a crown.*
Zechariah 9:16 (NLT)

Have you lost your sparkle?

What is your passion? What is the driving force in your life? Can you remember a time in your life when you exuded excitement over something, but perhaps you now find yourself discontented, broken, bored, or hungry for something more?

I believe that God especially made women to SHINE! As great influencers, we were cut, like diamonds, to shine and reflect the love of God. God desires to use your unique gifts, talents, and interests to shine His light into a broken, dark world.

Maybe you have lost your sparkle. That's okay. It happens to the best of us. Life sets in. Busyness, hurt feelings, and distractions suffocate the once-held passion that permeated all that we were. Or perhaps you don't remember ever having this God-shine in your life. Maybe no one ever helped you awaken your heart to a purpose that changed everything.

It doesn't have to stay that way; you were created to SHINE! I love the wording found in Zechariah 9:16 (NLT): *"They will sparkle in his land like jewels in a crown."* This verse tells me that God likes bling. He isn't boring or dull; He likes to accessorize His Kingdom with a little glam: and that includes YOU!

We were meant to bring attention to Christ. We were designed and uniquely fashioned in our mothers' wombs. We were not just BORN; we were SENT. We have purpose, and that purpose is found in shining the love and life of Jesus to those who are hurting.

Shining for God doesn't require a Bible college degree or spiritual perfection. Right now, right here in your world (your school, your home, your family, your workplace), YOU have been SENT to shine. You can reach people whom I can't. You are the bling in the crown of the Father! You are what causes others to notice His beauty and desire a relationship with Him.

When we lose sight of our purpose to shine, through busyness, sin, or selfish distraction, the natural by-product is boredom, purposelessness, and depression. The remedy is easy: begin to shine again by finding your purpose in spreading the Gospel. Begin to see that God can, and will, use YOU (His beautiful jewel) to bring others to Christ.

Drawing attention to the Father often is as simple as a random act of love to someone who is being unlovable, a generous gift to someone in need, a kind word or text, stopping to pray for someone who is obviously hurting, or cooking a meal for a friend who is going through a difficult time. These are small things that can make a HUGE impact in the lives of others.

So today, brush off any residue that has you feeling cloudy or dull. Determine to live TODAY as if it was your last chance to shine the light of God! (Can you imagine if we lived every day this way?) I promise that you will find a renewed sense of luster and passion when you commit to shining brightly, right where you are.

## TODAY'S ACTION STEP

It's time to shine like holy bling! On this last leg of our journey, we are going to purposely live with spiritual eyes wide open and be a holy sparkle to those around who may need it. Throughout your day, look for those who may be hurting or having a hard day (even if they take it out on you). Ask the Holy Spirit to give you creative ideas for how to spread His love to those in your sphere of life. Let's start with a simple way right now: before you finish your quiet time, take time to send a heartfelt text to another woman you know who may need the encouragement. Then look for other opportunities throughout the day to make a small difference in someone else's life.

# DAY 29.
# Switching Treadmills

*And who knows but that you have come to your royal position*
*for such a time as this?*
Esther 4:14b (NIV)

When we moved from Louisiana to West Virginia to plant our church, one of the first things I did after settling in was to join the local YMCA. Although I *did* want to get fit after just having had a baby, my primary intention in joining this gym was to meet people who were far from Christ.

No, I'm not a super Christian. What I am, however, is someone with the firm belief that Christians are meant to be MISSIONAL. I believe that we are meant to live life ON purpose and WITH purpose.

I haven't always lived like this. Unfortunately, I have lived more of my life being me-centered than others-centered. I have often gotten so sidetracked with my own life, dreams, and ministry that I have missed the God-opportunities that were set before me to reach hurting people right under my nose.

About a month after joining the YMCA, on a morning in early November, I found myself running on a treadmill and watching House Hunters International. (I love that show!) Several minutes into the workout/episode, I noticed a girl about my age on one of the other treadmills in front of me. I felt a God kind of tug at my heart to get off the treadmill I was on and use the one next to her instead. At first, I hesitated. I was pretty interested in which apartment the couple on the show was going to choose to buy in France, and the statistics regarding how many calories I had burned were already stored in the treadmill I was on. Plus, I was (frankly) tired and wanted some alone time. Nevertheless, I reluctantly obeyed the tug in my heart.

Suddenly, church broke out in the YMCA and hundreds came to the Lord right then and there!

No, not really. Actually, she and I just had a normal conversation about dieting, kids, and working out. Then some creepy guy kept trying to hit on us and wouldn't let us finish our conversation. That was it. No crazy supernatural experience. *Just treadmill talk.*

In my head, I prayed for her as I went to get some water, asking God to touch her life and show her His love. Then, as I picked up my son from the gym daycare, I bumped into her again in the nursery. I asked the Lord, *"Okay, God. If I'm supposed to do something, have her ask me for my information, because I don't want to be too forward."* Sure enough, before the prayer even left my head to ascend to heaven, she had asked me if I was on social media. She sent me a friend request that week, and that was it.

Flash-forward several months later: I hadn't really talked to her much. She would sometimes like my posts, and I'd like hers. Then, out of nowhere, she messaged me and asked me to pray for her because she was having a hard time. So I asked her if she would like to have coffee.

A few days later, in a coffee house parking lot, the "girl on the treadmill" met Jesus.

After an hour-and-a-half-long conversation, she and I wept together as I led her in a very broken, very beautiful sinner's prayer. It was one of the most amazing things I have ever had the honor to be a part of.

*But what if I hadn't switched treadmills?* What if I had simply enjoyed my workout, found out which apartment the couple on the episode chose, did my stretches, and never stepped into this divine opportunity?

Which brings me to my point: How many God-interruptions do we pass by each day? Each week? When we see our Maker one day, how many moments will we realize that we have missed as He attempted to interrupt our days with His divine purpose?

We often quote the famous verse found in Esther 4:14 (NIV), *"And who knows but that you have come to your royal position for such a time as this?"* But what if in the context of our own lives, it read like this: *"Who knows but that you have come upon this treadmill for such a time as this?"*

What if our destiny and purpose are encased in simple, ordinary, quite un-fabulous moments of choosing to use our time for the purposes of eternity instead of our own interests?

This experience challenged me to live more like Christ lived. He "switched treadmills" quite often. *(For instance, He traveled out of His way to reach the woman at the well in Samaria, who later won her entire city to Him.)* Jesus was INTENTIONAL, MISSIONAL, and OTHERS-oriented. We should be, too.

My prayer is that God will open our eyes to see these moments when He desires to interrupt our plans with His own. After all, if something as simple as switching treadmills can mean the difference in the eternal destiny for someone, isn't it worth the interruption?

## TODAY'S ACTION STEP

Your challenge today is to actively look for "treadmill experiences", purposefully watching for people in your life who may be hurting. Take time this morning to pray that God will help you to live with eyes wide open to the needs of those around you. Repent of any self-centeredness that may be creating a preoccupation that is keeping you from being aware of divine interruptions. Ask God to put people in your path this week who may be hurting or far from Christ, and then empower and embolden you to start a simple conversation, serve them in some way, or bless them with a random act of kindness. Believe that you can make an eternal impact in those around you when you are intentional, missional, and others-oriented.

# DAY 30.
# Washers, Dryers, & the Christmas Spirit

*They sold their property and possessions
and shared the money with those in need.*
Acts 2:45 (NLT)

Several years ago, my washing machine decided to bite the dust—three weeks before Christmas. Three clothes-wearing children (at the time), *plus* one broken washing machine, *plus* one hectic Christmas schedule, *equals* one hot mess!

My first thought was, *Fabulous. Just what we needed right before Christmas!*

My immediate solution to our washing machine problem was to do what we have done every other time an appliance in our home has broken: hit up the newspaper for the cheapest thing we could find, buy it, and use it until it broke down, too.

In our entire marriage, my husband and I had NEVER bought a new washer and dryer. We have always used hand-me-downs, trade-ins, or online yard sale steals. Granted, they usually didn't last more than a couple of years, but who wants to spend big money on something you throw dirty underwear into? Plus, our last set had been a great find, an unusually newer model that had lasted a long time. I could think of a million other great places for our money to go. A brand-new washer at Christmastime? I don't think so.

My husband, however, graciously vetoed my online yard sale decision. He had grown tired of the decade-long hand-me-down washer/dryer song-and-dance. He was ready for a commitment in the world of laundry, ready to finally stop our ten years of procrastination and stalling. Ready to purchase a new washing machine, once and for all.

Even though I HATED spending money on a brand-new washing machine at Christmas *(did I already mention how much I hated it?),* I reluctantly submitted to my better half and ventured out into the world of shiny, fabulous, NEW washers and dryers. We were blessed enough to find a steal of a deal in a new washer/dryer combo, half off in the scratch-and-dent section at our local appliance store.

I finally embraced the idea of settling down with my new friends, Mr. ShinyWhiny Washer and Mrs. Fancypants Dryer. I reveled in the idea of enjoying a cup of coffee while dropping undies in my energy-efficient, modern appliances.

Things got even better when the appliance store said they would give us free delivery and haul away our old washer and dryer. Good riddance and thank goodness! We didn't own a pickup truck, and I was a little worried we would end up with one of those houses where old broken washers and dryers became permanent lawn fixtures.

But as we walked back to our car, my husband asked me to get on social media and offer our dryer to friends who may be in need. I appealed to his common sense: "Why not just let the appliance store deal with it in the morning, and that way we know we won't be stuck with it if no one wants it?" He compassionately insisted that we give it away to someone who was in need.

I hesitated.

I began imagining my front porch adorned with an old dryer decorated with Christmas lights every year and stuffed with toys donated by my small children. *But I don't want a dryer as a landscaping feature! What if no one needs it? It would be so much easier to just let the appliance store haul it off and be done with it!* And yet, being the good wife that I am...I obliged and posted to my social media wall that we had a free dryer for whoever might need it.

Within MINUTES, my in-box was filled with requests.

I immediately realized how selfish I had been. I felt broken about those in need whom I had to turn away because the dryer was given away so quickly. The family who came to pick up the dryer actually went to church with us. They are sweet friends of ours, with two small kids of their own. They had been going to the local laundromat to dry their clothes for two months (since their own dryer broke and they had been unable to replace it). It was so awesome to be able to bless them and to be a part of the solution for a need in their life.

And to think I almost missed that blessing and gave their dryer away to the appliance store!

This incident got me thinking. How many things are collecting dust in my house that could be an answer to the prayers of someone I know? How many times have I accumulated things in excess while someone near me silently went without? Did I have a talent or a skill I could share with a family in need?

In Acts 2:44–47 (NLT), it says this about the Church: "*And all the believers met together in one place and shared everything they had. They sold their property and possessions and shared the money with those in need. They worshiped together at the Temple each day, met in homes for the Lord's Supper, and shared their meals with great joy and generosity—all the while praising God and enjoying the goodwill of all the people. And each day the Lord added to their fellowship those who were being saved.*"

Do you see the connection between a sharing spirit of the people in God's Church and the lost being saved? This is no coincidence. People encounter God's love not through a sermon, but when practical needs are met.

I can't help but look at that passage and think that many in the Church have forgotten why we were called a "city on a hill." I believe God never wanted the poor to have to become dependent on the government. The government is assuming a role that God intended for the local church to fulfill. We have a biblical mandate to feed the poor, clothe the naked, visit the prisoner, and take care of widows and orphans. Scripture even calls this "true religion" (see James 1:27).

I think that sometimes we erroneously believe that fulfilling this mandate to reach the hurting requires huge acts of self-sacrifice, when oftentimes it simply comes from random acts of generosity. Simply choosing to give away rather than to sell. Simply choosing to extend an open hand instead of hoarding. Cleaning out your closet, buying someone else's meal, fixing someone's car—this is how we show His love.

That Christmas, I became thankful for my broken washing machine. It broke my heart again for what matters to God...people.

## TODAY'S ACTION STEP

Are you willing to be inconvenienced enough to meet someone else's need this week? Do you believe that one random act of kindness can change lives? Prove it by taking time to go through your house and find an item or two to give away to someone you know who may need them. (Extra points if you still love and want to keep this item!) Use the gift of giving to inspire yourself to keep an "others-ness" mind-set.

# DAY 31.
# When Is "Enough" Enough?

*I have learned the secret of being content in any and every
situation.*
Philippians 4:12b (NIV)

A few years ago, after a two-and-a-half-year search, we finally purchased our first home. Prior to finding that house, we lived in a nine-hundred-square-foot apartment. As I sat locked in my tiny apartment with three kids during the long West Virginia winters, I would often daydream about what it would be like to have a large house where someone could sneeze without hitting another family member. We prayed for a LONG time for God to supply what we needed, and He so faithfully exceeded our expectations!

And yet, in the months following the purchase of our long-awaited dream home, I quickly realized how easy it would be to allow that big, beautiful blessing to become a distraction and a burden if I wasn't careful. Endless projects, painting, decorating, cleaning, repairs—they could consume my mind and my thoughts if I let them.

How ironic is it that blessings can sometimes distract us from the Blesser?

To this day, I have to make a conscious effort to turn off my brain and spend quality time with my kids. I have to let projects go unfinished while I have my quiet time with God. I have to be okay with a messy house on occasion and just enjoy spending time with my husband, realizing that the HOUSE is not what makes a HOME.

I know someone who has a beautiful, big home in a large metropolitan city. This family is very wealthy. From the outside, their life looks picturesque. As a matter of fact, when my kids first saw their home, my young daughter's reaction was, "Why are we so poor?" Ha! But behind those walls of perfection, I saw the eyes of a wife who rarely sees her husband because of the hours he must work to keep up with their lifestyle. I saw children who do not really know their father, and a father who does not really know his children. I saw hurt, emptiness, and pain as the backdrop of their family portrait, and I wondered, *Is it worth it?*

Proverbs 17:1 (NLT) says, *"Better a dry crust eaten in peace than a house filled with feasting—and conflict."* In our busy, materialistic world, there is great pressure to "keep up with the Joneses." This doesn't only manifest itself in our houses, but it can take form in how we look, what we drive, what we wear. It's the never-ending pursuit of perfection. But when is it enough? Will we have lost all that is sacred and eternal, all that really holds any lasting value by the time we reach "enough?"

The apostle Paul wrote, *"Godliness with contentment is great gain"* (1 Timothy 6:6, NIV). Philippians 4:11–13 (NIV) says, *"I have learned to be content whatever the circumstances. I know what it is to be in need, and I know what it is to have plenty. I have learned the secret of being content in any and every situation, whether well fed or hungry, whether living in plenty or in want. I can do all things through him who gives me strength."*

In the parable of the sower found in the Gospels, Jesus even cautioned His disciples about the dangers of allowing the Word of God to be "choked out" by the distractions of this world. He said, *"The worries of the world, and the deceitfulness of riches, and the desires for other things enter in and choke the word, and it becomes unfruitful"* (Mark 4:19, NASB).

Today I challenge you to evaluate your own home. Are you robbing it of peace in your pursuit of perfection? We cannot get our days back. Once they are spent, they are gone forever. If we are not careful, we will waste these days on things that will not hold weight in the light of eternity.

Let us purpose in our hearts not to allow our blessings to distract us, our goals to define us, or our pursuits to rob us from what really matters. Let's determine to keep Christ first and to love lavishly those whom God has placed in our lives. In a world where enough is not enough, let's realize that loving God, and loving people, simply is.

## TODAY'S ACTION STEP

Take time to look at your calendar. If what we value most determines where we invest our time, what does your schedule say about your priorities? Begin to pray over your week. Ask God to align your schedule with what He values and help you to remain on task. Write down any areas of perfectionism that are robbing you of joy and ask the Lord to help you find contentment right where you are. Determine that simple obedience to God's will is all that you need, and that Christ alone is enough.

# DAY 32.
# No One Likes a Brat

*Shouldn't I feel sorry for such a great city?*
Jonah 4:11b (NLT)

No one likes a brat. And yet we all have met them: little kids who make spectacles of themselves in the checkout line of the grocery store because they didn't get the toy they wanted.

I'm convinced there is nothing so humiliating to a parent than a child who throws a public temper tantrum. Almost every child goes through a stage when they test their parents to see if lying down on the floor and kicking and screaming will get them what they want. They figure out pretty quickly whether or not this bad behavior works.

While every *child* will try the tantrum technique, most people find it very disturbing when they watch an *adult* act like this. You know what I'm talking about: that lady (or man) who goes irate at the cashier at the fast food restaurant because her chicken sandwich was grilled and not crispy. *Can you say, "Awwwwkard?"* It's just embarrassing for everyone around.

While today's me-centric culture has bred an entire generation of adult tantrum-throwers, Scripture is not exempt from people like this, either. The Bible is replete with stories of grown-up brats. Even God's children *(dare I say it?)* and even God's PROPHETS have acted like spoiled brats! And I'm sure that God is just as embarrassed and frustrated when *His* children act like this as we are when *our* children do!

Which brings me to my point: Jonah was a brat. I'm sorry if this offends you, but it's my die-hard opinion.

I am a church kid, mind you. Growing up in the church, I have participated in musicals about Jonah's story, have been taught numerous Sunday school lessons about Jonah, and have created my fair share of children's crafts that tell his story. But as long as I can remember, whenever I was taught the story of Jonah, it was always a story about second chances. *Really, though, that is not at all the point behind his story.* When you read the book of Jonah in its entirety, you'll find that it actually revolves around God's preoccupation with and Jonah's resistance to one thing: saving a city living in spiritual darkness.

Sure, there are other things we can learn from Jonah's life, but the book as a whole is actually about God aligning things, supernaturally, to reach a people who were far from Him.

Throughout the book of Jonah, the phrase *"God-arranged"* pops up several times. We see that God arranged:

- A message for the city
- A commission to His prophet
- A storm to discipline Jonah (saving other lost people in the process)
- A fish to swallow Jonah
- An order for fish-expulsion
- A second commission
- A leafy plant to grow
- A worm to kill the plant
- A scorching wind

Over and over, the book of Jonah says the words, "God arranged" for each of these things to happen. Then, finally, in the last verse of the book, we get a glimpse into the heart of God behind all of this divine ordering: God said, *"But Nineveh has more than 120,000 people living in spiritual darkness, not to* mention all the animals. *Shouldn't I feel sorry* (i.e., have compassion) *for such a great city?"* (Jonah 4:11, NLT)

The book of Jonah is not really about its namesake. It's about God's compassion moving Him to save a lost city and His desire to use Jonah as a part of that process. Tragically, Jonah's infantile reaction distracts us from realizing this; his behavior is so normal to our own culture today that we barely notice how immature and appalling his attitude is.

In Jonah 4:2b-3 (NLT, emphasis added), Jonah blows me away with this statement: *"Didn't I say... before I left home that you would do this, Lord? That is why I ran away to Tarshish! I knew that you are a merciful and compassionate God, slow to get angry and filled with unfailing love. You are eager to turn back from destroying people. JUST KILL ME NOW, LORD. I'D RATHER BE DEAD! I'd rather be dead than alive if what I predicted will not happen!"*

Um... What?! God had just saved an entire city!

As annoying as Jonah is, his tantrum doesn't sound that far off from what I (or maybe even you) have said and done before, if we are willing to be honest. How many times have we been so caught up in our own lives, our own ministries, our own worlds, our own comfort, and our own dreams that we have missed sight of the plan of God to reach our cities for Christ? How many times have we pouted, sulked, rebelled, or run away when God's plans didn't work out the way we had in mind? How often have we lost sight of the fact that we are a part of something much bigger than ourselves—the saving of the lost through the Gospel of Jesus Christ?

Yes, God will send storms in our lives, send "fish" to put us in time-out, take away our plants of shade, as well as our comfort and provision—all to get us off of the floor from our tantrums and see that life is NOT, in fact, all about us.

Throughout time, God's heart has been beating for one purpose: *"to seek and to save that which was lost"* (Luke 19:10, NASB). How tragic would it be to stand before Jesus at the end of our lives and realize we completely missed the mark of His divine intention? How sad to realize we wasted time on things temporal, fading, and unsatisfying, while people we love now spend an eternity separated from Him? May this never be the case!

Let's not be so self-consumed in our desires, our lives, and our plans that we miss God's heart for our cities! There are thousands of people every day who are waking up around us living in spiritual darkness—hurting and broken. Right now, God is arranging, aligning, and moving circumstances on their behalf, to reach them with His great love. Even more beautiful, God desires that YOU be a part of His great rescue plan!

If God's heart beats so much for our communities, shouldn't you and I also feel compassion for our cities? If spiritual apathy has distracted you, ask God to give you His heart for the lost. Choose to take the attention away from yourself and begin to pray for those around you. Make the decision today to align your heart with what God is doing on behalf of the lost in your community.

## TODAY'S ACTION STEP

Read the book of Jonah. (Don't worry—it's only four chapters!) Write down any of Jonah's bad behaviors that you may not have noticed before. Do you see yourself in his actions or attitudes in any way? Take time to pray for your community throughout the day and ask God how you can be a part of His rescue plan for your city.

# DAY 33.
# God's Secret Weapon

*So they rushed back from the tomb to tell his eleven disciples –*
*and everyone else- what happened.*
Luke 24:9 (NLT)

Have you ever heard a piece of information that really needed to be kept a secret (like the fact that a friend is pregnant), and it almost killed you to keep it inside? That's a dumb question. This is a women's devotional book. Of course, you have heard a secret and couldn't wait to share it!

It's considered a high prize in the World of Women to know something FIRST. And once the secret is out, most women feel the incessant need to let everyone know, "I knew it first!"

Women are talkers by design. We have the gift of gab, the anointing for conversation, the talent for talk. We all know this can get us into trouble sometimes (don't worry, this isn't a devotional on gossip), but our love of sharing exciting news can also be a good thing. Dare I even say that it can be a "God-thing"?

After Jesus was resurrected, He did something amazing for His day and age. At the time of the life of Christ, women had little rights, often seen as no more than a man's personal property. A woman's testimony was not even valid in court. Yet, as He frequently did, Jesus shattered the status quo. He chose to commission a group of women to be the first to share the good news of His resurrection. Jesus appeared to Mary and several other women before He appeared to anyone else.

A group of women.

Why do you think that is? I believe it's because Jesus knew that if you want a piece of important information out fast, you tell the women! Read how Luke records what happened: *"So they rushed back from the tomb to tell his eleven disciples—and everyone else—what happened. It was Mary Magdalene, Joanna, Mary the mother of James, and several other women who told the apostles what had happened"* (Luke 24:9–10, NLT).

I love how it says that they told the disciples and *"everyone else"* what had happened! There was no need for social media, viral videos or live streaming to get the news out that Jesus was alive. All He needed was a few excited women!

Over and over, Jesus used unlikely women to quickly spread the good news of Christ. I believe that women are God's secret weapon in the sharing of the Gospel. We are His unsuspecting, often unnoticed, hidden weapon of choice against the kingdom of hell.

One of my heroes in the Bible, the woman at the well, won her ENTIRE CITY for Christ, simply because she encountered Jesus, got fired up, and then told people to come and see.

Do you realize the influence of your voice? Maybe today you don't feel like you have much of a voice. I realize that most of you are not preachers, teachers, book authors, or evangelists. But you are <u>chosen</u> to be His mouthpiece nonetheless! Never underestimate the power of your invitation, your encouragement, your voice! I believe that Satan trembles in his big, ugly boots when he sees a woman get excited about what God is doing in her life.

Between our online and physical campuses, the church we planted in West Virginia now reaches thousands of people on a weekly basis. We have seen hundreds come to faith in Christ, marriages restored, and addictions broken. We feed hundreds of starving children each day. We have a school in our community in which we provide a Christian education to the next generation. Each and every weekend, our altars are filled with people who are committing their lives to Christ—and all of this has occurred in less than five years!

But what amazes me is that before launching this church on August 19, 2012, our entire church could be traced back to ONE woman's invitation to a couple of other women to come to a Bible study we held at her house. That obscure Friday morning, only eight women showed up to a very modest morning women's Bible study. And yet what began as a spark flickered into a flame, as that small group of women brought their husbands, their children, told their friends, and together they BECAME A CHURCH!

Time and time again, we laugh as our women's nights are packed to capacity with a bunch of excited "God girls" who just can't help but share the Good News. And their invites are changing lives! Daughter of Jesus, don't EVER belittle the power of your own voice! Just because you can't see the fruit doesn't mean you aren't flourishing.

Today, I challenge you to send that encouraging text. Call that female friend who is hurting and pray for her. Post that invite to church. Tell that friend about what God is doing in your life. Don't let Satan ever douse your fire or make you think you can't make an impact for the Kingdom of God. Your voice matters, your enthusiasm is contagious, you are called, and you are chosen. You are God's beautifully fashionable secret weapon, and He's not afraid to use you!

## TODAY'S ACTION STEP

Take a step of faith today. Allow God to use your voice as His secret weapon against the enemy! Invite that coworker to church. Call or have coffee with that hurting friend. Share your story with someone. You are officially challenged to use your voice in some practical capacity today for the advancement of the Gospel. (It doesn't have to be "weird." Just pray, be yourself, and tell someone what God has done in your life.)

# DAY 34.
# A Different Way to Shine

*He did not retaliate when he was insulted, nor threaten revenge when he suffered. He left His case in the hands of God, who always judges fairly.*
1 Peter 2:23 (NLT)

Today I want to talk to you about a different way to shine your light before a dark world. This devotional will be distinctive from the others during this phase. We will focus on an often-overlooked, but highly effective way to use the life of God inside of you to reach the lost around you.

If you have committed yourself wholeheartedly to this 40-day ARISE Journey, you have by now undoubtedly seen the peace and fruit that accompanies radical devotion to Christ. But I also suspect you may be experiencing a more unwanted by-product of this commitment: *persecution.*

It doesn't take long to realize that not everyone will agree with the choices you make when you decide to dive all-in after Christ.

Jesus promised that your stance for God's Word would make you a target of hatred and suffering. He said, *"If the world hates you, remember that it hated me first. The world would love you as one of its own if you belonged to it, but you are no longer part of the world. I chose you to come out of the world, so it hates you. Do you remember what I told you? 'A slave is not greater than the master.' Since they persecuted me, naturally they will persecute you. And if they had listened to me, they would listen* to you. They will do all this to you because of me, for they have rejected the one who sent me" (John 15:18–21, NLT).

The Scripture is sprinkled from the earliest pages of Genesis all the way to the final pages of Revelation with stories of saints who endured misunderstanding, persecution, abuse, false imprisonment, hatred, and even martyrdom as a result of their radical obedience to God. As a matter of fact, a great deal of the Bible was written from a prison cell.

First Peter 4:4 (NLT) says, "*Of course, your former friends are surprised when you no longer plunge into the flood of wild and destructive things they do. So they slander you.*" I love how this verse says very casually, "Of course"—as if it should be quite expected.

If you are being mistreated, take comfort in a few things:

**1.** It is normal for the darkness to hate the light. (It is not personal.)

**2.** Scripture says we should actually be happy when we are mistreated for righteousness, because it affords us a heavenly reward: "*What blessings await you when people hate you and exclude you and mock you and curse you as evil because you follow the Son of Man. When that happens, be happy! Yes, leap for joy! For a great reward awaits you in heaven. And remember, their ancestors treated the ancient prophets that same way*" (Luke 6:22–23, NLT).

**3.** Persecution sets you up to shine the love of God with more intensity than ever before. Mistreatment can be our ally in sharing the Gospel; it can actually be a vehicle to carry the love of God to those far from Christ—*IF* we respond properly.

So, how can we use persecution to our advantage? Let's look at how Jesus did it:

*He (Jesus) was oppressed and treated harshly, yet He never said a word. He was led like a lamb to the slaughter. And as a sheep is silent before the shearers, he did not open His mouth.* (Isaiah 53:7, NLT)

*Then the high priest stood up before the others and asked Jesus, 'Well, aren't You going to answer these charges? What do You have to say for Yourself?' But Jesus was silent and made no reply.* (Mark 14:60–61, NLT)

*But Jesus made no response to any of the charges, much to the governor's surprise.* (Matthew 27:14, NLT)

*He did not retaliate when He was insulted, nor threaten revenge when He suffered. He left His case in the hands of God, who always judges fairly.* (1 Peter 2:23, NLT)

Did you catch that? Jesus had what I like to call an "anointing for silence." Simply put: *He kept His mouth shut.* He did not defend Himself, stand on His own rights, argue His side, rebut with scriptural justification, post passive-aggressive social media status updates, pitch His case before His friends and family members to get them on His side. NO! He "left His case in the hands of God, who always judges fairly."

I read a story just this morning about a time when the children of Israel were wandering in the wilderness, growing restless and angry with God. They decided to vent their frustration on Moses, Aaron, and the Levites (the chosen priests). After angrily approaching and falsely accusing Moses and Aaron of a number of things, the people challenged their validity and authority to lead at all. These hateful men felt they could run things better, and they questioned the motives of righteous Moses and his pals.

This angered the Father and burdened the Levites. But rather than asking God to smite them, Moses pleaded for mercy on their behalf. He loved them anyway. He and Aaron kept their mouths shut and just prayed. This left room for God Himself to defend them.

God instructed Moses and Aaron to have each tribe (including the Levites) present a staff, representing their tribe, in a holy showdown of sorts. He said, *"Buds will sprout on the staff belonging to the man I choose"* (Numbers 17:5, NLT). The next day, this is what the tribes of Israel discovered: *"When he went into the Tabernacle of the Covenant the next day, he found that Aaron's staff, representing the tribe of Levi, had sprouted, budded, blossomed, and produced ripe almonds!"* (Numbers 17:8, NLT)

God vindicated Moses and Aaron without them having to say a word.

Here's my point: If we leave things alone and just trust God, the fruit will speak for itself over time. People will be able to see the results of our integrity and righteousness via the good works we produce, the miraculous hand of God on our lives, the peace in our homes, and the blessings that naturally bud from a life that is rightly connected to the Source of Life.

If, however, we become distracted and engaged with our persecutors, that connection to the Father that produces light and life is diminished. In our efforts to defend ourselves, we instead discredit ourselves and prove our accusers to be right. We take our eyes off of the goodness of God and lose the Source of love and peace.

Sister, you can rejoice in the fact that if you are being persecuted, you are also simultaneously being poised to demonstrate the tangible love, forgiveness, longsuffering, and mercy of Jesus to those who are watching! Yes, it requires restraint. Yes, it requires an "anointing for silence." Yes, it requires deep, agape love. Yes, it PUSHES YOU TO JESUS, because without Him you can't love like that!

Persecution can be a setup for a miracle, if you choose to do it God's way. If you take the humble road. If you are patient and let God be your defense. It might be a different way to shine, but it is also an effective one!

## TODAY'S ACTION STEP

If you are feeling misunderstood or under attack, take time right now to pray for your accusers. Ask the Lord to help you have an "anointing for silence" and trust in His ability to be your defense. Today, every time a thought tempts you to defend yourself or become angry with that person, instead stop and pray for them. Ask God to give you a burden and a love for those who mistreat you, so that you can shine the light of Christ in this different, but beautiful way.

# DAY 35.
# Shining in Suffering

*Most important of all, continue to show deep love for each other,*
*for love covers a multitude of sins. Cheerfully share your home*
*with those who need a meal or a place to stay.*
1 Peter 4:7–9 (NLT)

My second-born child, Zia, was sick as an infant. Very sick. She averaged half of each month in the hospital, and almost every day was a fight for her life. Suffering from a rare form of bone marrow failure, she experienced many moments when we weren't sure whether she would live or not. It was a dark time. It was a time I look back on now and wonder, *"How did we make it through that?"*

Interestingly, Zia means "light." God gave us her name very early on in my pregnancy. We didn't know whether she would be a boy or a girl, but as soon as we saw her, we knew this name fit her so well. In the months that would follow her birth, it became more and more apparent just how prophetic that baby's name was. She was a little light in a very dark place.

Because bone marrow failure is a blood issue, St. Jude Children's Affiliate in Baton Rouge became her primary care facility. They specialize in childhood hematology (diseases of the blood) and oncology (cancer). They are amazing! We loved the whole team, and they became like family to us. We shared holidays and birthdays in the hospital, late nights and early mornings, setbacks and successes. It was a journey we will never forget.

Thankfully, the Lord miraculously and spontaneously healed Zia when she was three years old! Her little light fought hard and won against the darkness that had tried to snuff it out. I firmly believe that what she went through was preparation for where she is going. I feel deeply that her suffering forged a compassion that will fuel her calling later in life.

But looking back, I'm thankful that we didn't wait until Zia was healed to begin to use our suffering as a chance to shine the light of God. Oh, it would have been very easy to hyper-fixate on our pain, our trauma, our fears. Many would say we would have been justified to do so. But God taught us early on in that journey to *look around when we are hurting*. To find in every dark place an opportunity to shine His light.

The "St. Jude wing" (as we called it) of the hospital was a place that needed light. When we were tempted to implode beneath the weight of our own dark circumstances, we could just simply peek down the hall of that hospital wing. There, we would find children much worse off than Zia. Children with stage-four cancer. Single moms with multiple children hospitalized at once from sickle cell anemia. Families fighting for the lives of their children apart from the hope of Christ or the support of a home church. Nurses who bore the weight of a very difficult job, serving very sick kids and their grieving families.

We realized that even in our suffering, it was selfish to hold on to the light when others sat in darkness. We discovered the joy that is found in ministering IN and THROUGH our pain. We found that our difficult road gave us credibility to speak into the lives of those whom many other people could not.

So we prayed in midnight hours, walking halls with exhausted mothers. We blessed families with care packages and money to help with expenses. We helped bury kids who did not make it.

We cried. We loved. We did our best to make the most of this horrible sickness. We forced Satan to pay for making our baby suffer.

First Peter 4:1–2 (NLT) says, "*So then, since Christ suffered physical pain, you must arm yourselves with the same attitude he had, and be ready to suffer, too. For if you have suffered physically for Christ, you have finished with sin. You won't spend the rest of your lives chasing your own desires, but you will be anxious to do the will of God.*"

Friend, if you wait until you don't have troubles to shine your light, the enemy will make sure you continue to have one fight after another! Please understand that while it may be tempting to crawl into a hole and hide in times of pain, you are actually in a position to shine the brightest during your darkest hour. Don't miss the profound fulfillment that comes from arming yourself to suffer and anxiously accomplishing the will of God in the midst of your trial.

The rest of that epistle says this: "*The end of the world is coming soon. Therefore, be earnest and disciplined in your prayers. Most important of all, continue to show deep love for each other, for love covers a multitude of sins. Cheerfully share your home with those who need a meal or a place to stay*" (1 Peter 4:7–9, NLT).

I find it beautiful and interesting that a chapter on suffering includes commands such as sharing "your home with those who need a meal or a place to stay." This command is a key to finding purpose in your hurt. One of the most powerful weapons we have against depression is the weapon of outreach. No one will ever be able to convince me otherwise! Something miraculous awakens in the heart of the downtrodden when they take their focus off of themselves and begin to serve and love others who are hurting.

I'll never forget when my little miracle baby was in kindergarten, she bee-bopped into the house after school one day and announced proudly, "Mom! I know how to find joy! It's JESUS, then OTHERS, then YOU! If you do things in that order, you can have joy!"

What a profound revelation for my five-year-old little sunbeam. Boy, was she right!

I'm fairly certain (and thankful) that Zia doesn't remember those long hospital nights, the multiple surgeries, or the pain of her sickness. She has no recollection of the bedsides of dying babies, the beeping of IVs, or the smell of a sterile hospital wing. But something beautiful was deposited in her spirit during that time. She learned to serve others even when she was hurting. She learned that no amount of darkness could dim a light that was determined to shine. She learned the recipe for joy in the midst of pain: JESUS, OTHERS, YOU.

## TODAY'S ACTION STEP

Begin to pray for those around you. Ask God how you can use your suffering to open opportunities to shine light in the darkness. Journal the names of those in your sphere who may be hurting or broken. How can you practically serve or bless them this week? Try to take the focus off of your current circumstances and find the joy that comes through an others-centered life.

# DAY 36.
# Hey There, Darlin'

*Charm is deceptive, and beauty does not last; but a woman who fears the Lord will be greatly praised.*
Proverbs 31:30 (NLT)

My great-grandmother was a baby-making machine. She had fifteen children! I am told that all fifteen kids slept on the floor of a one-bedroom shotgun house in the tiny town of Drew, Mississippi. We called her Mammaw Parttridge.

Mammaw Parttridge was very short and round, with lots of spunk. Back during her baby-making years, it was taboo to talk about being pregnant. Her kids said they wouldn't even know she was expecting until she would miss a day out in the cotton fields. The very next day, she would be found outside picking cotton in the southern sun, with a new baby strapped to her chest! Now, *that's* a strong woman!

Oh, how I loved that woman. Every time we would visit her old, crooked-floored house, she would greet me with a kiss on the cheek and a raspy, slow, very Southern, *"Hey, there, darlin'."*

I can still remember the sound of the cold box fan in the room I slept in when we stayed at her house. I remember her washing dishes and me almost being as tall as she was (even though I was just a child). I remember the comfort of her squishy arms wrapped around me. *"Hey, there, darlin'."*

Not only could my great-grandmother physically procreate like a champ, she did so spiritually, too. I was just a child when she died at the ripe old age of eighty-five, but I remember her funeral well. To this day, I have yet to attend a funeral quite like hers. Usually the elderly do not have large funerals. Most of their friends and loved ones have already passed. But on that warm afternoon in southern Mississippi, close to four hundred people filled the church to celebrate the life of an eighty-five-year-old homemaker.

I remember overhearing bewildered adults, wondering where so many people had come from. Then story after story of her quiet impact began to be told. Although racism was rampant at that time, horrifically tolerated, and segregation was expected, she shattered the norm and loved across colors and cultures. She took in the downtrodden, fed the hungry, and housed the orphans.

*"She took me in when I had nowhere else to go." "She helped me get back on my feet." "She helped raise me."* These were the stories of her many, many spiritual children. Over and over again in that room, I heard impersonations of her Southern *"Hey, there, darlin',"* followed by tears and soft giggles.

I'm so proud to have her as a part of my spiritual lineage. No, she never published books, started a nonprofit organization, owned a Fortune 500 company, or started a viral YouTube channel. She just loved one person at a time as they came across her path.

Mammaw Parttridge multiplied herself physically and spiritually. I am here today as a result of her decision to follow Christ. (And her decision to have lots of babies!) Her choices forever affected my life and the lives of my own children.

And she did all of that from a crooked Mississippi kitchen floor.

I am proud to have her story as a part of my legacy. Proverbs 31 describes a woman of virtue—a woman like my Mammaw. It accurately predicts the end result of woman who lives her life in fear of the Lord.

*Charm is deceptive, and beauty does not last; but a woman who fears the Lord will be greatly praised. Reward her for all she has done. Let her deeds publicly declare her praise.* (Proverbs 31:30–31, NLT)

Do you want to have a legacy that outlives you? I know the greatest reward I could ever hope for would be a spiritual inheritance to leave to my children. My highest goal in life is not to attain some crazy celebrity Christian status. I just want to produce an abundance of spiritual fruit, birthed out of love and an intimacy with the Father. I want to reach the end of my life knowing that I did all I could to love people and reach them with the Gospel of Christ.

When I get to heaven, there's only one thing I want to hear more than my sweet great-grandmother say, *"Hey, there, darlin'."* And that's the voice of Jesus, saying, *"Well done."*

## TODAY'S ACTION STEP

Hey there, darlin'! Maybe you're tempted to think you aren't making an impact. I pray my great-grandmother's story inspires you today to continue to be faithful in small acts of great love. Continue to look for ways to be a blessing to your family, your neighbors, and your community.

# DAY 37.
# This Little Light of Mine

*Do not neglect to do good and to share what you have, for such
sacrifices are pleasing to God.*
Hebrews 13:16 (ESV)

Have you ever had someone come into your mind or heart and
then coincidentally bump into them while out and about? Have
you ever been asked to pray for someone who is having a tough
time and then remember that you had meant to check on them
just days earlier, but had forgotten? Has an idea of something
nice to do for a friend popped into your head, but busyness
prevented you from following through? I think we have all been
guilty of this.

*But isn't it the thought that counts?*

Not really. At least not according to Scripture. I want to spend
today briefly discussing a practical, simple way to make a big,
eternal impact. I would like to awaken you to a crazy thought:
perhaps our good ideas, our concern for certain friends, and our
happenstance run-ins with others are not so "coincidental" after
all. Could the Holy Spirit actually be prompting us to shine our
little light without us even realizing it?

What if mistaking the person in traffic next to you for an old
friend may actually be God's way of nudging you to remember
that person in prayer or call to check on them? What if shining
our light doesn't have to be so complicated or irregular, but what
if it rather simply required a small amount of effort and follow-

through? Could making a big impact be as straightforward as choosing to act on our good intentions?

James 4:17 (NIV) says that *"if anyone, then, knows the good they ought to do and doesn't do it, it is sin for them."* If we take Scripture very literally, this verse can be pretty convicting. Hebrews 13:16 (ESV) says, *"Do not neglect to do good and to share what you have, for such sacrifices are pleasing to God."*

According to Strong's Concordance, this word "neglect" in the Greek means "to lose out of mind; by implication, to neglect." It only implies neglect. Its more direct meaning is "to lose out of mind," or more simply, to forget. Scripture encourages us not to lose sight of our mandate to do good with modest but impactful acts of love.

When I moved from Louisiana to West Virginia at the age of twenty-eight, it was an intense time in my life. In many ways, it was like the death of the only life I had ever known up to that point. As we said our emotional good-byes, many of my friends, family members, and even some casual church acquaintances wrote me letters telling me what I had meant to them. It was strange. Almost like attending my own funeral.

I was very surprised to hear all of the little things that had made tremendous impacts on the people in my life. Many of these things I did not even remember doing. Things like writing a heartfelt thank-you note after my baby shower, thoughtfully telling the person what they meant to me, instead of an easy "thanks for the diapers." Things like stopping a few minutes to pray for someone in the grocery store or at the altar in our church. Simple things that really didn't take much of my time, but that proved to be so worth it.

It encouraged me not to trivialize small acts of kindness. It made me desire to "remember" to shine my light in as many little ways as possible.

Today, if you think about someone, pray for them. If a sister or a friend is on your heart, text her or call her. If you have an encouraging word for your husband, your child, or a leader, say it. Take a meal to the friend who had a baby. Stop by the hospital to visit the sick person you know. Help someone who's moving to unpack. Throw a small baby shower or plan a get-together for someone who may need it. Drop off a gift card to the one who is struggling. Have coffee with that friend you have been meaning to catch up with. But be careful to do it before you forget!

I suspect we may be surprised when we get to heaven and hear which aspects of our lives made an eternal impact. Jesus promised that even a cup of cold water wouldn't go unnoticed in eternity. So don't hide your light or ignore the Holy Spirit's subtle promptings; let your little light shine for all to see!

## TODAY'S ACTION STEP

Pay careful attention this week to the times when you think of a friend, family member, coworker, or even a stranger with compassion. Take the time to stop and pray for them, text them, or bless them in some other way. Purpose to follow-through with the "God ideas" that pop into your mind and watch how God can use you to shine your little light!

# DAY 38.
# Breaking the Fourth Wall

*Go and announce to them that the Kingdom of Heaven is near.*
Matthew 10:7 (NLT)

In acting, there is a term called "breaking the fourth wall." In theater or on television, there are two sidewalls of the set, one back wall, and an invisible "fourth wall" where the audience views the play or show. Both parties are aware that there is nothing really separating their worlds except their imaginations. Sometimes, however, an actor may "break" this "fourth wall" by speaking to the audience directly. It can be done by accident (perhaps an actor is startled by a sneezing audience member) or intentionally, but it is usually not preferred.

I believe Jesus was a fourth-wall breaker. Jesus Christ, the Son of the Living God, who hung the stars and the moon, who has numbered the hairs on your head, who told the waves of the oceans how far they were permitted to go onto the shore—this Jesus—SHATTERED the fourth wall of humanity when He was born two thousand years ago.

He continued to break the fourth wall as He forced people to acknowledge that there is another realm that exists parallel to ours, which is called the "Kingdom of heaven." He acknowledged that the Kingdom of God had come, and we should acknowledge it, too.

Most people are aware (whether they choose to admit it or not) that there is a supernatural realm around us that we ignore every day. Some people live hooky-spooky lives that are obsessed with the supernatural. They are fascinated with horoscopes, psychics, ghosts, and the like. (By the way, the Bible is clear that these things are evil and a dangerous trap of the enemy. Christians should *never* take part in such things, as they will open themselves up for demonic influences.)

Other people pretend there is nothing more to life than the here and now. Science and human reasoning are their gods. They struggle to find meaning in life, because apart from Christ there is no meaning.

But I believe most of us happen to fall into the category of just being distracted by the here and now, forgetting that our days are actually being spent on eternity.

*Tick-tock. Tick-tock.* We are counting down until our expiration date on earth is reached. The God-given destiny and purpose on our lives is either being fulfilled in His Kingdom or squandered on things that have no eternal value. Many people are uncomfortable with those who, like Jesus, shatter this fourth wall. When "radical" Christians address the Kingdom of God among us, it makes others nervous. But too much is at stake to play pretend and ignore the inevitable eternal consequences that await each of us.

I believe that graveyards are filled with dead destinies—those of talented musicians, singers, pastors, missionaries, doctors, mothers, and fathers who WASTED that precious, indispensable, invaluable commodity called TIME on things that ultimately did not satisfy their souls.

Jesus was constantly prodding humanity to acknowledge the Kingdom of God. He put it this way: *"For whoever wants to save their life will lose it, but whoever loses their life for me and for the gospel will save it. What good is it for someone to gain the whole world, yet forfeit their soul? Or what can anyone give in exchange for their soul?"* (Mark 8:35–37, NIV) Again, you can hear His sense of urgency when He commissions us to *"go and announce to them that the Kingdom of Heaven is near"* (Matthew 10:7, NLT).

Today, let's examine our lives with honesty. The Bible says that our lives are like a vapor. This small fragment of time in which we exist is an investment in our endless eternal state. Once we live out our days, there will be no turning back. How are you living your life? Are you living for the eternal or the temporal? When your eyes meet Jesus' eyes, will you hear the words "well done"?

Humanity is on an eventual, inevitable collision course with eternity. God will one day permanently shatter any invisible fourth wall that separates your world from the eternal. Whether by the end of the age or by the end of our days, we will all be forced to acknowledge there is more to life than the here and now. This is an inescapable fact that frames the entire story of the Gospel. The show is winding down, the plot is coming to a climax, and when the curtain falls, we will each stand before a holy God who will wholly make us give an account for how we lived out our part of this Great Story. We do not have to wait for time to break the fourth wall, we can choose to live eternally minded each day. Let's determine today to make Jesus the Star of the show and live "the rest of our days as the best of our days" for His eternal purposes.

## TODAY'S ACTION STEP

Today, I pray that you can sense the urgency and importance of God's commission for you to spread the Gospel and spend your life on His eternal purposes. Take time to ask the Lord if there are any specific ways you can make an eternal impact. (For example: volunteering at your church in a greater capacity, increasing your financial giving to your local church for the advancement of the Gospel, beginning a ministry or a work that has been on your heart, reaching out to a hurting neighbor or coworker, etc.) Have the courage to be a fourth-wall breaker in your sphere of life.

Embrace the nearness of the Kingdom of God and then watch the way it purifies your motives, increases your passion, and fuels your intentionality!

# DAY 39.
# A New Journey Begins

*Do not despise these small beginnings, for the Lord rejoices to*
*see the work begin.*
Zechariah 4:10a (NLT)

We are nearing the end of our journey together. In the first few pages of this book, my desire was to awaken you to the hope that you CAN get up from anything. As we entered the Arise Phase, we shifted from merely a mental and emotional journey to a practical one, as we put weight to the inward work God has been doing with concrete life applications. Throughout this Shine Phase, I pray that God has brought you from a place of healing to a place of purpose. My prayer is that you now realize that God has called you up and out of the mire for a reason—that "arising" is the doorway to an abundant life and not the finale. It's the beginning point of another amazing journey still ahead of you.

In some ways, then, although we are finishing our ARISE Journey together, you are back at another starting point: a launching pad for a new season—and it's an exciting one!

I love fresh beginnings. New things, bold ideas that are pregnant with possibility.

But new beginnings can also be overwhelming. Maybe God has put a dream in your heart and you hear His emphatic call to "Go!" and make disciples. Perhaps you see a way to impact eternity in your own sphere of life—to help the downtrodden, to minister to the orphan, to right injustice, but you feel inadequate, ill-equipped, or a little overwhelmed. You know God is calling you to do *something*, but you don't know what, how, or with what means you have even to start.

Moses was in a similar situation when God called him to greatness. He had a laundry list of excuses as to why he could not accomplish the task that called to him from the burning bush. God, discontent to leave Moses alone with his excuses, asked, "What is that in your hand?" and Moses answered, "A shepherd's staff" (Exodus 4:2, NLT). So, armed with only the call of God and a stick, Moses began the work he was called to do.

This story repeats itself over and over. David took down Goliath, not with Saul's heavy armor, but with five stones (*what was already in his hands*). When the crowds were stirred as they listened to John the Baptist preach about the Kingdom of God, they asked what they should do. John replied, "If you have two shirts, give one to the poor. If you have food, share it with those who are hungry" (Luke 3:10–11, NLT).

A stick. Some rocks. One extra shirt (probably a V-neck, multi-cotton blend). A leftover Chick-Fil-A sandwich. These are the ingredients of miracles.

We find out in Zechariah that God loves small beginnings. He gets tickled over His kids taking bold steps of faith with little more than what's already in their hands. He challenges us, "*Do not despise these small beginnings, for the Lord rejoices to see the work begin*" (Zechariah 4:10a, NLT).

This word "despise" in the Strong's Concordance means "*to despise, hold in contempt, hold as insignificant.*" It's tempting to belittle what's already in our hands, to roll our eyes at our seemingly insignificant pile of rocks and wonder, *What am I going to do with this? How can I change the world, my community, or even my home with THIS?*

I've written some about our big move to plant a church here in West Virginia. It was a dream in our hearts for ten years. When our pastors agreed, and we finally felt that the season was right, we were on cloud nine. We piled into the car and drove nine hundred miles to move into a nine-hundred-square-foot apartment, sight unseen, with our family of five. We had big, bold dreams of a life-giving, thriving church that would reach this hurting community in a radical way. We couldn't wait to get started!

But the honeymoon was short-lived.

After two months of living in West Virginia, we felt alone and inadequate. There were several people we knew from the community whom we had assumed would be part of the launch team of the church. However, upon moving here, those people did not feel it was the season for them to be a part of a new church plant.

I remember very vividly sitting in our tiny living room one evening as my husband got off the phone with one such family. They had lovingly and honestly expressed that they didn't feel the timing was right and they broke the news that they could not be a part of our team. My husband hung up the phone, sighed, looked at me, and said, "Well, baby, I guess THIS is I Heart Church," as he pointed to our three kids and me.

A wave of fear came over me for an instant. *We uprooted our family and moved nine hundred miles from our home! We are supposed to start our services in four months, but we have no money and no church team! How are we supposed to accomplish this, God? Did we miss You on this one?!*

"*I guess THIS is I Heart Church.*" Two broke adults, a second grader, a kindergartener, and a newborn. *Fabulous.*

But almost as quickly as the doubt came, so also a voice of faith rose up inside of me. "It won't stay that way," I said. And as I opened the Bible in my hands, the first verse on the page was this:

> *The smallest family will become a thousand people,*
> *and the tiniest group will become a mighty nation. At*
> *the right time, I, the Lord, will make it happen.* (Isaiah
> 60:22, NLT)

Less than four years later, this was our reality. We were running over one thousand attendees on the weekends, and daily watching God top Himself as families were restored to Christ, the addicted were being saved, and hearts were made new in Jesus. Although the journey was not easy, and although it required every drop of blood, sweat, tears, and faith we had, we started with what God gave us and God made the impossible, possible.

We determined simply to be faithful with every person whom God put in our path, beginning with our kids. Then we poured all we had into the couple whom we met at the coffeehouse, the Mexican restaurant, the eight ladies who showed up to our home Bible study. And as we were faithful with the few, God gave us many.

Today, the church we see with our physical eyes is even more amazing than what we saw with our spiritual eyes years ago. God has exceedingly, abundantly filled our cup to overflowing, and we are really just getting started! But it began with simple obedience with what was already in our hands. When I look back those days of big, scary faith in that tiny, dark apartment are some of my favorite memories. They are a testimony of what God can do, and how "little is much, when God is in it."

So, if you are asking where to start as you prepare to close the pages of this book and begin the next beautiful, bold journey you will take with the Father, the answer is simple: Start with what's in your hands. It may not be much, but it's enough.

## TODAY'S ACTION STEP

Has God placed a dream in your heart? If this is a Kingdom dream (meant for spreading the Gospel or serving others), God desires that you step TOWARD it in some way! It doesn't have to be radical or extravagant. It could be as simple as taking a care package each month to a family in the hospital. It could be as modest as collaborating with a few friends and bringing warm food to the homeless. It may look like volunteering at church or at a nonprofit organization, or hosting a free yard sale in an impoverished community. Take roses to the nursing home. Bake cookies for veterans. If you are a mom, then you can *and should* involve your kids in this process!

Perhaps your dream is to write a book—so just start with page one! (I strongly suggest connecting your dream to other organizations, especially your local church. We are better together, and there is strength in numbers and accountability.)

Remember, you will not be held responsible before God for what you *didn't* have, but rather what you do! God is cheering you on, rejoicing to see your work begin. Don't belittle what is in your hands, but rather, deposit it!

# DAY 40.
# Broadway and Wall Street

*Teach us to realize the brevity of life, so that we may grow in wisdom.*
Psalm 90:12 (NLT)

A few years ago, my oldest daughter and I went on a school field trip to New York City with her fifth-grade class. It was my first time in New York (outside of the JFK and LaGuardia airports, anyway). We visited all of the normal touristy places as a group: the Empire State Building, the Statue of Liberty, Times Square. We also visited the 9/11 Memorial. But my favorite part of the trip was when we were able to break away from the group and explore the grounds of Trinity Church.

Trinity Church is located in a very unique spot: on the corner of the famous Wall Street and Broadway. It seems out-of-place and even otherworldly, its ancient architecture sticking out like a sore thumb against the modern backdrop. Although the original church building was lost in a fire, the cemetery and mausoleum that surrounds it can be dated back to 1697 (before America was even a nation!).

The cemetery morbidly fascinated me. My daughter begged me to leave it, to no avail. I circled every inch of the church, reading tombstones older than our country itself—imagining what life was like long before skyscrapers littered the sky with metal.

One thing that struck me was how young the majority of the buried were. This was a time when a sixty-year-old was considered "aged." Most of those buried in this famous cemetery were under the age of thirty at the time of their deaths. The tombstones are so old, many required careful deciphering, between the Old English language and the lettering worn by time and weather.

There I was, circling an old graveyard in the heart of NYC, when something stopped me dead in my tracks. My touristy, nerdish, semi-morbid stroll drastically turned into something more as I read the tombstone of an eight-year-old boy, buried many lifetimes ago, in the year 1793. This is what it said:

*In memory of Anthony*
*Son of Anthony and Elizabeth*
*Who died July 10th, 1793*
*Aged 8 years, 2 months and 20 days*


*Reader, reflect as you pass by*
*As you are now, so once was I*
*As I am now, soon You will be*
*Prepare for death and follow me.*

Is it just me, or did you just get the heebie-jeebies?

This isn't from a fiction novel. This is real! Right there in one of the most famous spots in the world sits this incredibly cryptic warning, calling out to millions passing by.

I couldn't help but wonder: *Why would a parent put this on their eight-year-old's tombstone?*

I firmly believe it was inspired by the Holy Spirit long ago. Before there was a stock exchange, before there were musicals, long before the hustle and bustle of NYC, when this land held just a field and a church, this boy's tombstone etched a prophetic warning: *Take heed how you live.* Here on the corner of Wall Street and Broadway (the world's stage of both money and entertainment), as millions hurry by in their hustle and bustle, the dead cry out to the living.

Psalm 39:6a (NLT) says, "*We are merely moving shadows, and all our busy rushing ends in nothing.*"

All our busy rushing.

How much time do we spend at the corner of Wall Street and Broadway, blissfully ignorant of the clock that ticks down to our expiration date? How long do we loiter around the idols of wealth and stuff, entertainment and comfort, wasting precious days that were meant to be invested in eternity?

This is why the psalmist prayed: "*Lord, remind me how brief my time on earth will be. Remind me that my days are numbered—how fleeting my life is. You have made my life no longer than the width of my hand. My entire lifetime is just a moment to you; at best, each of us is but a breath*" (Psalm 39:4–5, NLT).

Before you pin me as dark or gloomy, listen to what Solomon said in Ecclesiastes 7:4 (NLT): "*A wise person thinks a lot about death, while a fool thinks only about having a good time.*"

I realize that the topic of death is uncomfortable. But it is also inevitable. (New studies show a 100 percent mortality rate among humans—*wink!*)

We are each on a running timer, set to expire someday. Will your life count? In what will you invest your precious days? It's so easy to become distracted by stuff or by fun that we miss our assignment. But we are here on purpose. God desires to use you—yes, YOU—in His eternal, redemptive plan.

Do you see it? Can you feel that you were made for more than just existence?

You are so loved that God created you with INTENTION and forethought. He redeemed you and saved you. He called you to AWAKEN from the pit in which you were trapped, to ARISE to new life, and to SHINE with renewed passion and purpose—and it's a big one!

God can and *will* use you. You can finish your assignment and hear, "Well done!" but it will take living with intention and resolve. It will take grit and determination. It will mean choosing to stay free when the call of yesterday's addictions comes banging at your door. It will mean not just getting up, but STAYING UP TO FIGHT.

Make no mistake, if you are going to arise to your purpose, it will certainly be through bloodied knees, broken paths, and repeated failures. You will have to endure the screams of haters, the taunts of accusers, and the cries of naysayers. You will be misunderstood, mocked, exhausted, and ridiculed. There will be times when you want to give up and quit or turn around and go back, but hang on—because you CAN do this!

God is making your arms strong for this task (Proverbs 31:17), and He Himself promises to battle with you and for you (2 Chronicles 20:15). You are His!

Do you hear Him calling you? His voice is thundering from the pages of this book into the recesses of your heart. Right now, Jesus is calling you!

*Talitha kum! Girl, I say to you, "ARISE!"*

Congratulations on finishing the ARISE Journey! To watch a special online conclusion message from the author, visit arisejourney.com/afterthejourney.

# CLOSING PRAYER

Father, I thank You that You loved your daughter so much, that You pursued her and called her to time aside with You during these forty days. I ask You, Holy Spirit, to seal the work of God that has been done in her heart and to see it to completion.

God, You know the enemy would love to undo what You have done, to rob her from the fruit produced by continuing in Your Word. So, I pray as she reads these words that You would protect her and cover her, dispatching angels to war for her and surround her. I ask You, Father, to embolden her by the knowledge of Your extravagant love. May she abide in You every day, becoming more like Your Son.

I ask You to use Your daughter for a mighty Kingdom work. May she rescue the hurting and defenseless from the mouth of the enemy. I pray she will fearlessly stand up against injustice and courageously go where You tell her to go. I pray she never looks back. May she so radically follow You, that she makes hell tremble!

I pray Your girl will hit the mark of the high calling of God in Christ Jesus and produce exponential fruit that remains. May she meet you face to face and hear, "Well, done." And may a generation of righteous daughters follow close behind her. In Jesus' Name. Amen.

# Review Request

Thank you so much for taking the 40-day ARISE Journey! Now that you've read this book, if you enjoyed it, then please let other readers know. Let's share the knowledge and help other women to awaken, arise, and shine in their God-given potential!

# About the Author

Photo by Nichole Meadows, Frozen Moments Photography
frozen-momentsphotography.com

Melodi Hawley is a speaker, women's pastor, and mom of four. She and her husband Brandon Hawley founded I Heart Church in Beckley, West Virginia, and now pastor this vibrant, growing church. Melodi has a passion to use the Word of God (combined with humor and transparency) to empower women to rise up from any circumstance. She uses this passion for God's daughters to fuel the annual ARISE Women's Conference, which equips women from all walks of life to live victoriously through Jesus Christ.

To learn more about I Heart Church, or to watch online sermons from Pastors Brandon and Melodi Hawley, visit iheartchurchwv.org.

# Arise Women's Conference

The ARISE Conference is an annual event hosted by I Heart Church, under the direction and vision of Melodi Hawley. The ARISE Conference exists to empower women to rise above any circumstance or obstacle through the power of Jesus Christ and His Word!

Designed to be a life-changing weekend experience full of practical biblical teaching, worship, creative media, and artistic expression saturated in a dynamic, fun atmosphere, the ARISE Conference is open to all women age eleven and up, from any background or denomination.

For more information on the next ARISE Conference or to find out how you can attend, visit arisewomensconference.com.

# Author's Acknowledgments

The completion of this book could not have been accomplished without the support and encouragement of the beautiful people of I Heart Church, my family and my friends. I am thankful for my many sister/friends who enabled me through their time and physical assistance to finally pen what God wrote on my spirit years ago. I am also immensely grateful and indebted to the many who contributed to my own personal journey of freedom that led to the writing of this book. I could in no way adequately express my gratitude to all of those who have encouraged me along the way, but I would like to give particular mention to the following:

My husband Brandon, for pulling me out of the destructive pit I had fallen in and being Jesus to me at my worst. You, more than anyone, have taught me what grace means. Thank you for helping me to hear the call of my Savior to "arise" and then being my champion in the years that followed my freedom. Thank you for encouraging me to write when I thought I couldn't, for supporting me late at night when I was exhausted, and for your relentless prayers. Thank you for dreaming bigger for me than I ever could have and for calling me your Proverbs 31 girl so much, that I started to believe it. You're my knight in shining armor!

My "big girls", Eden and Zia, for babysitting, cleaning, and praying for your mom so I could finish writing. Thank you for never resenting God's call on our family. Thank you for believing in your mom and being so excited about this project. It meant the world to me that my girls had my back. I can't wait to do the same for my future world changers!

Jennifer Minigh, for selflessly walking me through every step of the publishing of this book with the single-minded goal of impacting God's Kingdom. Thank you for seeing this with eyes of faith long before I did and planting that seed in my heart years ago. Thank you for your beautiful heart to share God's Word through print and to empower others on their journeys to that dream becoming a reality. This book would have never happened without you. I am forever grateful.

Delynn Rizzo, for the years you and Pastor Dino invested in Brandon and me, both personally and as a church, and for, of course, contributing to this book with such a precious foreword. Thank you.

My parents, for their constant support and prayers, not just during the time of the writing of this book, but for as long as I can remember. I love you mom and dad.

Pastors Mark and Cindy Stermer, for your patience and wisdom. Thank you for being our spiritual parents and never leaving us as orphans. Thank you for restoring me and not leaving me in my own shame, for loving me beyond my depravity, and then pushing me to get up and shine the light of Jesus to a world that needs it so desperately. This book is a part of your fruit.

Nichole Meadows and Savannah Grimmett, thank you for the time you gave so that my vision for the cover of this book would be so perfectly realized.

Jesus, my beautiful Savior, for rescuing me and cleaning me, restoring and redeeming me, calling and empowering me. I long to see You face to face and hear You say, "Well done." May this book bring pleasure to Your heart.